The World's Bestselling Program **and Solution**

# ZOMBIES FOR
# Zombies

## ADVICE AND ETIQUETTE FOR THE LIVING DEAD

**By Your Host**
# David P. Murphy

### Illustrations by Daniel Heard

**SOURCEBOOKS, INC.®**
NAPERVILLE, ILLINOIS

Published by Sourcebooks, Inc.
P.O. Box 4410, Naperville, Illinois 60567-4410
(630) 961-3900
Fax: (630) 961-2168
www.sourcebooks.com

Library of Congress Cataloging-in-Publication Data

Murphy, David P.
  Zombies for zombies : advice and etiquette for the living dead / David P. Murphy.
      p. cm.
  1. Zombies—Humor. I. Title.
  PN6231.Z65M87 2009
  814'.6–dc22

                              2009013968

          Printed and bound in the United States of America.
            CHG 10 9 8 7 6 5 4 3 2 1

# TABLE OF CONTENTS

# ACKNOWLEDGMENTS

To Mom and Dad: for always allowing me to be my goofball self.

To Bill and Bethie: for teaching me how to make fun of the world.

To Cindy and Dylan: for any number of perfectly good, loving reasons.

Daniel Heard: my eternal thanks. You truly helped bring this book to, uhhhhhh, life. You're an amazing talent and a helluva co-host!

Laurie Fox: more gratitude than you'll ever know. I wouldn't have had this opportunity if not for your belief and tenacity. You're a peach of the highest order, a true inspiration and friend.

Thanks also go to Linda and Gary at the Linda Chester Agency.

Peter Lynch: thank you so much for a smooth and completely pain-free experience. Your enthusiasm for this project has meant a lot to me (but concerns me nonetheless). And thanks to Carrie and everyone else at Sourcebooks for all of their efforts.

Dr. Theodore Anfinson: so very kind of you to help in the medical realm. You're as astute, brilliant, and hilarious as ever.

To my friends, for their support and comic abuse over the years: Henry, Pat and the kids, Curt and Meg, Mitchel and Marisol, Scott and Donna, Tom and Heather, Queenie, BobbaGutz, Joannie, Sheila, Charlotte and John, Faye, Peter and Pamela, Anita, Rhonda and Rick, NenaGutz, Samarama, Barb and John, Waggs, Julia, Dee, Justin Heard, Wingy, Tony M., Jenn Dorn, Scottie, Keifsk, the Milone tribe, MichaelGutz, Marla, Frances, Karyl, Kerry, Casey, Michael and Jennifer, the Great Ether, Gung, Diane, the Morins, and everyone else who ever bought into my hairbrained schemes.

And, of course, to every zombie and post-lifer everywhere: this world is a little more beautiful and a lot more sluggish with you in it. Mmmmmmwah!

*All the people like us are we, and everyone else is They.*
—Rudyard Kipling

*I said to a bartender, "Make me a zombie."*
*He said, "God beat me to it."*
—Rodney Dangerfield

# FOREWORD

## BY DR. KENNETH BEAKER

I've been told there's a recommendation of some sort regarding the reader getting through this book in roughly seventy-two hours. So perhaps it would be best for all concerned if I make my comments as brief as possible. This does not, however, indicate any lack of appreciation on my part for *ZOMBIES FOR ZOMBIES*™; the book and program have been, shall we say, rewarding.

In the troubling years that followed the initial outbreak of the Provo Virus and its subsequent tragic effects, there was little hope for those like you, knee-deep in the Transition™. During those early days, the infected's options were limited to being taken to church, being whisked away to the nearest Holding Ranch (later to become Containment Zones), or enduring countless hours of poking, testing, and/or sales training. You see, in those days, no real plan was in place to help those in need; no system had been devised that could offer the proper amount of hope. And perhaps worst of all, no medications had been developed that could be given an appropriate markup.

I'm happy to report that those initial deficiencies are a thing of the past. As a result of the outstanding work done by many folks (including, might I add, myself), there is now a united front in dealing with the "just-infected." An important aspect of this improved effort is what you're reading now. That's why it gives me great pleasure to introduce you to this wonderfully inspiring book, *ZOMBIES FOR ZOMBIES*. Alas, restricting its potential in any way by referring to it as "just" a book does it a disservice, because *Z4Z* is part of a vast, innovative strategy designed to help those in the midst of the Transition retain as much of their humanity as possible. If we're going to one day reclaim our world from the bloody clutches of the Horde™ and experience civilization at its finest again, it's imperative that *Z4Z* becomes an integral component of your recovery process.

Oh yeah, the time limit. I'll wrap up my remarks now.

Nowhere else will you find such a voluminous amount of info regarding your immediate future. Nowhere but here will the quality of guidance offered be more spot-on. Almost every given feature of your radically revised life is addressed in what you hold in your clammy hands. Hold it tight, my friends, hold it tight.

Okay, so now some suit from QualiCorps™ is all over me about the time constraints. Just chill.

In *closing*, let me say how very honored I am to be included in this project and grateful to the author and all the corporations, individuals, and corporate individuals who work tirelessly on behalf of those in the Transition. You've made what's left of our world a far better place.

Godspeed, dear reader.

There. I totally rushed it. Ya happy?

Dr. Kenneth Beaker
Author of *Everyman (for Himself)*
Maui Safe Area #5

# INTRODUCTION

So you've been bitten by a zombie. Bummer.

The first thing to remember is not to panic. Yes, your life will be undergoing a major transformation, but this doesn't have to be the end-all it once was when the Disaster first hit. There have been significant breakthroughs in the last decade (in large part due to the efforts of QualiCorps) in assisting people with keeping bits of their wit and dignity. Together, I assure you, we *can* limit the damage. This book will make a profound difference in your accidental strange new life. All is not lost. However, make no mistake, *something* is.

*ZOMBIES FOR ZOMBIES*, among other things, is a motivational guide that has been designed specifically with you, the recently bitten, in mind. You say you don't want to become another one of those ghastly creatures you see on the news out in the Tempe Containment Zone? That's right: you *don't*. As you know, *they're* the Horde and they are, as sociologists say, *icky*. They're the ones who were infected in the first two years of the Disaster; hence, those nasty beasts were never given a chance to benefit from a program like this.

You, on the other hand, don't have to end up like them and/or morph to that degree. Granted, over time, you *will* lose large parts of your vocabulary and perhaps a few teeth, but hey, that's true even for folks in the Ozarks. First things first: read this book like there's no tomorrow, because in your case tomorrow isn't what it used to be.

If you *have* been recently bitten (or infected in any other manner), start reading this NOW. Stop thumbing through this at the local bookstore cafe, sitting on the floor and freaking out about your little wounds. Get off your butt, put down the freakin' chai, and go *pay* for this book. You'll be *really* glad you did. Time's a-wastin' and so are certain types of cells. According to our latest scientific results and marketing tests, if you get through this book within *three days*, you'll be far more likely to retain a modest degree of your higher functions and cognitive abilities.

## SHOULDN'T I BE AT A HOSPITAL?

You can take that route. Feel free. I can tell you, though, what will happen: you'll sit in the E.R. for hours as a jaded medical attendant tries to get your bioscan right while another drone pours over your Identidocs. You'll be made to fill out an endless amount of paperwork and submit to a government-mandated retina test.

You see, everyone's still trying to get it right in dealing with the chaotic aftermath of the Disaster. As a result, there's a crapload of red tape and jangled societal nerves. So at some point that same attendant will be in the middle of extracting the fourteenth vial of your blood, and you'll suddenly start feeling feverish and queasy. You'll begin to wonder why you even bothered with the hospital and what the hell the co-pay is for a visit of this magnitude. Ten? Ninety? Twelve-hundred? Is this even covered in Section 18 of the Preferred Procedures Masterlist? And while you're obsessing about such details, three dudes in hazmat suits will suddenly show up, sedate the heck out of you, and lead you away to a Halfway Region.

So it's time for the dirty truth: there's no cure. Not at the hospital, not anywhere else. No Panglossian version of your current state here. The Transition has begun and there's no stopping it. You can, however, *slow it down*. Way down. It can be decelerated enough for you to have a shot at a semi-normal post-life. This is what *ZOMBIES FOR ZOMBIES* can do for you if you let it.

## IT'S SO NOT ABOUT ME

Right about now, you're probably asking yourself, "Who is this author anyway and what's he about?" In response, I'll say this: it's not about me; it's about *you*. You're the one in need. Still, to quell your fears, I'll tell you that I'm just an average Joe who's seen a number of friends and family members fall to the Provo Virus. As a result of this, I've been deeply affected. Matter of fact, these losses made such an impact on me that performing community service on behalf of post-lifers™ became a passion of mine. I logged literally dozens of hours at the nearby Scarlet Shores™ facility, playing piano and Yahtzee and smoking with the staff. What I learned from these experiences fills this book. So here's my pledge to you: you're going to get the help you need during the Transition in order to understand what's happening to you.

## NAVIGATING THROUGH Z4Z

Inside Z4Z, you'll find helpful tips on a wide range of topics:

- How to dress for your new lifestyle
- Great tricks for getting bloodstains out of your clothes
- Handy recipes for brains
- Deep stuff concerning spirituality
- Fitness ideas for keeping you toned and somewhat energetic
- New skin-care techniques to help ward off "rotting flesh syndrome"
- Proper grooming
- How to overcome that darned zombie social stigma
- Dance steps for the motor-impaired
- Handy recipes for brains (yes, I know I'm repeating myself, but soon you'll be showing a lot more interest in brains)

To get the most out of *ZOMBIES FOR ZOMBIES*, be advised that along with the use of text boxes and sidebars (such as the one on the next page), icons will be employed to emphasize salient points and remarkable products and, conversely, steer you away from concepts that suck. Examples of icons include:

 Important points to remember, if at all possible

Negative ways of thinking or behaving/products to avoid

Yiddish for no apparent reason

Liquor

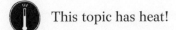 This topic has heat!

 Spiders!

$ Financial advice that could lead to bags of money or stamps

☠ Pirates!

🕐 Hurry up and read!

## STILL NOT SURE IF THIS BOOK IS FOR YOU?

If you continue to have doubts about whether you need this book, please review the following checklist to determine which, if any, of these situations might apply to you:

One quick note about the format of this book: whenever you see a sidebar like this with the symbol above (no slobbering), please take a moment to read it. These sidebars will always underscore a valuable insight the book is making.

## INFECTION CONFIRMATION CHECKLIST!

YES ☐　NO ☐　Have you ever been bitten, scratched, or mauled by any known Provo Virus carrier?

YES ☐　NO ☐　Do you have a strange wound that's turning dark green and you don't know where it came from?

YES ☐　NO ☐　Have you recently been on a cruise ship?

YES ☐　NO ☐　Have you been sweating excessively? Do you reek of sulfur and not know why?

YES ☐　NO ☐　Did you, at any time within the last several weeks, take one of those subversive "Club Z Vacations" to a Containment Zone?

YES ☐　NO ☐　Has your tongue turned blue?

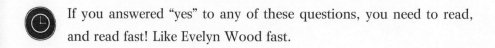 If you answered "yes" to any of these questions, you need to read, and read fast! Like Evelyn Wood fast.

## STICKING IT TO THE NUTJOBS!

Before we go into high gear, I think it's important to address an ethical issue that you may have heard being discussed by your homeys or in the media. Some particularly fanatical fringe activists have argued that the post-life setting you'll enter into is a sham and is merely a fiendish method for controlling a catatonic and decomposing populace. This is a cynical and pathetic viewpoint. Having witnessed what my friends and family went through during the Transition and how various groups assisted them in their times of need, I can unequivocally state that Z4Z is only a small part of a larger system that has at its center one purpose: compassionate service. It's the intent of everyone involved—the Shores, big pharma, and all the other groups and companies that comprise this post-Disaster "structure of solutions"—to provide comfort and care. And yes, maybe there is a modest profit now and then, but does that mean said profit is undeserved or that it negates all the good that's being done? I think not. So until there's a cure for the Provo Virus, we will forge ahead, kindly and confidently, in the direction of that service.

Unless your last name happens to be "van Winkle," you've got to be aware of how dramatically our world has changed in the last decade or so. Nothing is how it once was, and it's going to be quite awhile before our culture returns to normal. In the meantime, it's imperative for you to know that all of us—every race, creed, and color—have been impacted equally. The Provo Virus has no sense of prejudice or preference. Once infected, you're going to be in the same boat with everyone else in your condition, and unless you let Z4Z (and its affiliates) help you, that boat is headed toward one big-ass iceberg. And you won't be king of the world.

Bottom line: the age of discrimination is over. There is only one *them* now and it's the Horde. To that end, we will need all the unity and solidarity we can muster. Consequently, there's no longer any good excuse for harboring ill will against your fellow man.[1]

## OKAY, CAN WE GET BACK TO MY SPECIFIC SITUATION NOW?

Of course. Let's *do* talk about your situation. Life may have handed you a lemon from hell, but that's no reason to pucker up your face in such an unsightly way. (Oh, sorry—that's one of your symptoms.) *Z4Z* will enable you to move past every major physiological and psychological hurdle and get you back on track.

Now, if you happen to be younger than sixteen, I recommend that you immediately put down this book and pick up the delightful companion book, *ZOMBIES FOR ZOMBIES FOR KIDZ!*™. *Z4Z4K!* offers you a wide array of enlightening games, brain-buster puzzles, and cutesy stories along with guidance camouflaged as "fun." And not to worry: if everything works out as it should, you'll end up at Scarlet Shores Jr.™, which is not unlike a colossal camp for kids who are in the Transition. Cool digs, killer grub, and each day packed with activities galore. Weaving! Sewing! Making clothes for foreigners! With the monthly sanctioned Visiting Days with your friends and family, you'll almost feel like you're home.

Meanwhile, for those of you who *are* adults, be aware that there may be times when it appears that this book is little more than a veritable catalog, hawking page after page of products for those in the Transition. Appearances, however, can be deceiving. Remember, *Z4Z* is committed to introducing you to the best items on the market to enhance your health and vitality. Additionally, from time to time you'll be made aware of free

---

1. Although those Rosicrucians *still* make me cranky.

offers from multiple merchants. Said info is mere frosting on the cake; the bulk of this book remains devoted to furthering your cause so that you can continue to be a vital part of our society and economy.

## FUTURE'S SO BRIGHT...

It may be hard for you to believe right now, but once you've completed this book, you'll be at peace and may seem even *more* sophisticated than you ever were in your former life. As a result, you'll feel loads better about your situation. Eventually.

 So now that your panic attack has subsided, I'd say we best get started. Time is ticking; let's get shamblin'!

# WHO MOVED MY BRAINS?:

## THE PROVO VIRUS AND YOU!

You've entered the Transition. Through some unfortunate circumstance that's no fault of your own, you've been infected with the deadly Provo Virus. Here's what you need to know: from the moment of your initial infection to the conclusion of the Transition, you have approximately sixty-eight to seventy-six hours before you become one of "them"—the Horde. But as stated earlier, you're not going to end up as one of them. Trust me.

## DON'T KNOW MUCH ABOUT HISTORY

Let's roll back time a bit so as to better understand the epic story that led to your current condition. And not to worry—just because we're going to talk about zombies for a brief moment doesn't mean that's where *you're* headed. We're using the term freely here.

Zombies have a rich and colorful story that goes back many, many years. The Internet (because it *is* the most reliable information source ever known to man) tells us that belief in zombies began in Haiti decades ago with voodoo practitioners. There it was believed that certain magicians could bring the dead back to life while others were overly flummoxed by the old "milk into a paper cone" bit. If no current dead were available, it was decided the merely napping would suffice. In addition, many of those powerful Haitian wizards were also famous for passing primitive hoops around "floating" females. (Surprisingly, between reanimating the dead and the hoop trick, the native audiences consistently preferred the hoop.) Once the reanimation "took," the voodoo priests frequently returned the deceased to their loving yet horrified families. Alas, the resulting zombie silence at the dinner table was incorrectly attributed to ongoing household quarrels and not to catatonia.

Who knew? Catatonia is not a state in the former Soviet Union but, apparently, an altogether different sort of state. It turns out that catatonia is one of the many symptoms of being a zombie and defined as "an extreme loss of motor ability." Another characteristic of catatonia is that patients stay rigid for hours and ignore all stimuli.

It should be noted that it was in this catatonic state that zombies were often used as lackeys or flunkeys or, worst of all, flackeys. Chiefly utilized for slave labor by the Haitians, they were also exploited by being made to perform in embarrassing skits staged for rich white guys who resettled on little-known tropical islands with their buxom, beautiful, and helpless daughters. This slavish aspect of the zombie heritage has, in this author's opinion, been marginalized over the years to a discomforting extent. Little-known fact: it was zombies who were largely responsible for building the early Caribbean railway system, dozens of sugar factories, and a bitchin' water park outside of Les Cayes. I hope one day they get the credit they deserve.

Early versions of zombieness supposedly still exist in the Caribbean and certain parts of northern Georgia. However, our modern-day model (2.1 and counting!) is, of course, a direct result of the tragic and accidental toxic outbreak from the QualiCorps Labs in what used to be Provo, Utah. Shame about Provo. Pretty town in its day. And a mall to die for!

## PEPPERONI, ONIONS, AND EXTRA DEATH!

This brings us to the recent past and to the beginnings of the actual Disaster. The virus, it turns out, was not a virus at all, but a prion, a more primitive beast akin to Mad Cow, but way madder.[2] As you probably know, the Disaster was unleashed on the world in a tragic pizza delivery accident. To be completely fair, the prion was set loose by a research team working overtime at QualiCorps Labs *and* a pizza guy. Although details remain somewhat sketchy, that night a terrible screw-up occurred at the labs: a researcher, reaching into his pocket while distracted, inadvertently tipped the pizza delivery guy a couple of bucks and a vial of the deadly strain with which the team had been working. It was postulated that

Scientists have found that catatonia can be brought about in a number of different ways: 1) by ingesting *coup de poudre*, a type of terodotoxin like that found in the deadly Japanese puffer fish; 2) by Datura, an herb known to cause euphoria, even in Ben Stein; 3) by prolonged exposure to QVC; and, strangest of all, 4) by the victims believing that they have no will of their own, much like creationists.

---

2. After much heated debate, it was decided that referring to this outbreak as the "Provo Prion" wouldn't do. Such a moniker would lead to the abbreviated "P.P.," which sounded like something a three-year-old boy would say; not nearly scary enough. Hence, the inaccurately named, yet more effective, "Provo Virus" was coined, and that's how I'll refer to it going forward.

the driver returned to his truck, unknowingly compromised the vial's seal, and that was that.

The same evening, dozens of infected pizzas were delivered, along with apocalyptic crazy bread and buffalo wings of death.

Thus began the Disaster, the worst bio-outbreak in the history of the human race. Those who were infected quickly turned into zombies and stopped showing up for work (which certainly compromised their requests for disability). These folks became the Horde, and have proven to be not only unruly neighbors but formidable enemies as well. It took years and countless telethons[3] for the governments of the world to bring the situation under a degree of control. Even so, scientists were unable to find a cure, and as stated earlier, this situation continues to be the case. Gratefully, life has become a bit more manageable than it was at the height of the Disaster. Through the establishment of Containment Zones, Halfway Regions, Safe Areas, the Scarlet Shores Facilities, and, yes, the invaluable *Z4Z* program, slowly but surely society is returning to a more genteel existence.

## TRANSITIONEERS™, SAY "HELLO" TO YOUR PROVO VIRUS!

Let's not kid ourselves, though: even as you read this, the neurotoxins from the virus are racing through your system like pimped-out Roombas. Cells are mutating and croaking at an incredible rate, and your spleen has transformed into a substance resembling gelatinous Mountain Dew. Likewise, the vermis of your cerebellum is nothing special in the looks department and is currently fending off a hostile takeover. I wish I had better news, but that's how it is. Change is a-comin', and it's a-comin' on fast!

---

3. If you like Norm Crosby, it was a golden era.

Imagine the Provo Virus in action: a healthy blood vessel is hanging out, minding its own business and providing recreational shelter for an innocent group of capillaries. Suddenly the P.V. blows into town and, like a band of banditos, comes streaming in, looking for trouble. After an initial exchange of uncomfortable pleasantries with the good-natured capillaries, the separate strings of the virus get surly and close rank around them. Within moments the virus erects what appears to be a large, lovely event tent and invites the little capillaries inside, only to immediately consume them. Despite the festive appearance, it's a bloodbath.

Later, we find the virus displaying its hunger-driven white stage as it descends on a perfectly pleasant enough red blood cell. Without so much as a "how do you do," the white virus latches onto the cell and won't let go. The poor bastard of a cell never stands a chance and is fully engulfed mere seconds after our imaginary interlude begins. The P.V. is merciless, deadly, *and* efficient.

Now that you've got a rough idea of what's going on with your body, please study the following chart in order to better understand the chronology of the Transition.

| THE TRANSITION—A TIMETABLE OF YOUR DEMISE! | |
| --- | --- |
| Hours 0–10 | Initial wound becomes infected within moments and subject starts to sweat like Louis Armstrong at a rave. Provo Virus sets up booth in bloodstream and begins making "cold calls" to organs. Virus is a smooth |

| | |
|---|---|
| | talker, doesn't take "no" for an answer, and closes the deal with a free set of ShamWows. Tongue turns blue. |
| Hours 11–20 | Body temperature starts to escalate. Subject becomes overly sensitive to light and any comments concerning his/her weight. Whimpering can be heard. Certain patients describe a nasty metallic taste in their mouths while others crave Ho Hos. Toenails curl, knuckles swell. The word "pus" is bandied about. |
| Hours 21–30 | Dark rashes begin to break out all over the body, itching like a sonuvabitch. Pores start to secrete green, pasty substance that goes nicely with chips and salsa. The need to urinate constantly becomes an issue, even worse than at that kegger in Kenesaw. Muscles spasm, nostrils flare, and the letter $v$ disappears from the subject's "ocabulary." Fingernails loosen and uvulas burst. Ear hair grows exponentially. Ew. |
| Hours 31–40 | All rashes unite into one giant rash and vote to secede. Not good. Convulsions emerge as a new "pastime." The fever has most likely reached approximately 103 degrees, and subjects are swooning like boomers at a Bon Jovi concert. Simple conversation becomes difficult as jaw becomes harder to move, and mind begins to "downsize" while brain "outsources." Teeth turn dark yellow and gums brown. Unflattering. |

| Hours 41–50 | Major organs now resemble Wham-O products. Tendons are brittle, which depresses the heck out of most muscle groups. White blood cells have rented a POD, packed up, and moved to a friendlier locale. Don't even ask about the antibodies. Anger finally surfaces, particularly when the voice of Sean Hannity is heard. His brains, however, sound as if they could be porcine and tasty. |
|---|---|
| Hours 51–60 | Growling has begun in earnest. Skin is now a Ferrigno-like hue, and it's becoming more difficult to find the right clothes to complement this tone. Veins turn dark and protrude from the skin to a Stan Winston–like degree. Eyes, too, start to bulge and twitch in their sockets. Mucus flows like champagne at a hip-hop after-party. Surliness is substantially worse to the point of genuine unpleasantness. Subjects are officially "no longer fun to be around." |
| Hours 61–70 | An incredible hankering has developed for whoever's handy. Slobbering galore. Walking has become more difficult due to spinal compression, fallen arches, and sagging spirits. Communication skills have been replaced by emphatic groans and occasional scribblings on a whiteboard. Subjects can no longer recognize family or friends, which is not all bad when the doorbell rings at 2:30 a.m. |

| Hours 70+ | No data provided. The Transition is complete and you're officially toast. |
|---|---|

So why do you need this schedule? The answer is twofold: you should try to comprehend the biology behind what's happening, *and* you need to accept the *inevitability* of your evolution. The life you've had is going away quicker than a Cuba Gooding film, and a brave new existence is replacing it. While it's true you won't be quite the witty conversationalist you once were, you can, with a modicum of effort on your part, ensure that at least several of your consonants will remain available for your future use.

## NEUROPLASTICITY AND KEEPING UP WITH THE Qs

This radical change on multiple levels is why the first chapter is titled "Who Moved My Brains?" In your remaining time, or "tempus humanus" (as we professionals call it), you'll begin to experience a serious loss of cognitive skills and motor functions. This *will* happen soon, but take comfort in the fact that this loss is what is referred to as a "fixed-response reduction." It does not gain momentum in any way; it will not snowball on you. If you choose to do *nothing*, the effects of the Provo Virus will relentlessly drain you of your mind at a predetermined algorithm, leaving you with the personality of a Duraflame. But you're not going to do nothing; you're going to fight back.

Ironically, it's your very own brain that will do much of the heavy lifting via "neuroplasticity," your new best friend. Neuroplasticity is the brain's ability to remap information after an injury or damage has occurred. In other words, despite being pummeled by the Provo Virus, your brain (with a boost from *Z4Z* and its sister products) will actually rewire itself and move your most valuable "files" to a safe and secure location.[4] Fortunately for you, the exercises provided later in this chapter have been proven to assist the brain with this redistribution of data.

Along with offering an invaluable boon to neuroplasticity, this book also aids the process of "neurogenesis," which is the ability of the noggin to produce more neurons. More neurons means a speedier mental response to any given situation, and, jeepers, that's gonna prove helpful. By giving both of these neuro processes a quantifiable "goose," you'll be markedly better off, and your QScale™ number will most likely hover slightly between the categories of lesser primate and NASCAR commentator.

What's the QScale, you ask? Not so long ago, the U.S. government, along with researchers at QualiCorps Labs, developed a 1 to 10 ratings system for determining an individual's level of humanity. This QScale was meant to serve as a "measuring stick" to more accurately gauge the quantitative differences taking a toll on your system. Its intention was a natural response to the Disaster and eventually became an effective litmus test for determining how "Horde-esque" a given victim had become. For example, your typical Horde member would rate a 1 while an uninfected human would be a 10. As you can imagine, there's a lot of gray area between the two extremes, particularly if you ever worked at a law firm.

---

4. In order to achieve this, your brain needs the necessary time for the neuroplasticity process to kick in. See Chapter 3 regarding this.

For the sake of full disclosure, you should be aware of ongoing disputes among members of the scientific community about if and when the QScale might be applicable to the average non-Transition human. One side believes it's heresy to attempt to employ such a system in that manner, while the other believes that scientists should be free to rate *anyone*—e.g., Geraldo as a 5.3. This author offers no opinion one way or the other.[5]

Gratefully, there are numerous methods and new medications to help you keep your QScale number rising or, at a minimum, stop that nasty downward spiral. But be forewarned: you're probably already an 8.9 and sinking fast.

## ❧ A DELICATE BALANCE ❧

Silly me. Here's a symptom I forgot to mention: your inner ear is about to be trashed. To quote a doctor friend, the virus seems to "have the hots for Eustachian tubes." Fortunately, the degree of damage won't impact your hearing too dramatically, but it *will* screw with your balance. While you won't be falling down frequently, a simple walk will require a more focused effort as you learn to navigate with your now-crummy motor responses. To help deal with this situation, look for a valuable product called Ear-igate™ mentioned later in the book.

---

5. Although a 5 does seem generous.

# IT'S SORT OF LIKE BEING A TEEN AGAIN!

Analogy time: remember during your teenage years how your hormones raged and every other morning you'd wake up with a fresh zit or three? Your body was changing quicker than Bobby Brady's voice. Think of the initial phase of the Transition like this but far more dynamic. In the next several days, you'll be witness to a mind-blowing series of events and changes in your body that will make zits seem like a hangnail.

But wait. Remember how, when puberty *did* arrive, life went on and the zits went away?[6] You'll have a similar experience with the Transition. Shortly, you'll return to a state of calm and normalcy, and all those awful memories of the day you were bitten will seem like nothing more than a bad dream. Your hormones may still continue to rage every now and then, but they can be kept at bay utilizing Romerin (see Chapter 3) and by maintaining a positive outlook and an urbane persona.

# LEGAL CH-CH-CH-CHANGES

No discussion about your rapidly evolving condition would be complete without addressing your new legal status. After the Transition is complete, you'll be escorted to whatever Scarlet Shores compound you've been assigned. Not to worry. The Shores (as they've come to be known) are akin to impressive and elegant assisted-living (or post-living, if you will) facilities where you'll reside, dine, and shop. But here's the nitty-gritty: once you've been welcomed and processed, you'll lose your right to vote and to own property (unless it's vacation land you purchased from that nice Erik Estrada).

Additionally, you'll need to surrender your driver's license; in its stead, you'll be issued a shimmering new identification card as part

---

6. And Bobby started singing like Josh frickin' Groban.

of your revised Identidocs. You won't be needing that driver's license anymore anyway, because you won't be allowed to drive. That's right, no more cars for you. (Make plans now to give your car away to someone you love. Personally, I wouldn't donate it to one of those screwball do-gooder charities; they'll just sell your sweet ride for a marginal tax break.) But before you go all nuts on me about this news, think of the perks: no more auto insurance, no more repair bills, no more tickets, no more pain at the pump, and no more court appearances because you "tapped" that old dude in the intersection while you were texting your bff.

Are you starting to realize this isn't all bad? Your transportation needs will be completely taken care of, and you won't have to do diddly. For the full 411 on this, look for info about ShuffleCrafts later.

So other than these three strikes against you—no voting, no property, no sweet ride—there will be no other major changes to your personal liberties except that your freedom of speech will go down the drain, too. But what the heck—like you ever used that!

## SHOOT THE TIME CLOCK

When it's been determined that you haven't "gone Horde," post-life will be much like your old life with plenty of time for fine dining, relaxing, and endless hours of quality TV. One big difference for you, though, will be that you won't need a job anymore. You heard me right—this is how retirement was meant to be. Your only time obligation will be to contribute fifteen hours a week of community service (i.e., tidying up), for which you'll be paid in the seven stamp categories (Food, Liquor, Drug, Beauty, Tobacco, Garment, and Cable). Your consistent commitment to service will enable the Shores to stay spick-and-span, and the stamps will allow you to still play a vital part in our struggling economy. Additionally, you'll be required to show up at any of your Shores' local InfusoHuts for your weekly plasmapheresis session, where your bad-to-the-bone blood will be replaced with the remarkable artificial blood product, Hemo-Glowin™. This process is painless and a little like dialysis for your circulatory system, but far more enjoyable.[7] So other than the infusions and those fifteen hours, your time is yours to use as you see fit. Where do *I* sign up?

## NO BRAIN, NO PAIN

Intelligence is overrated. How often do you read on the Tubes or hear on the Telly about a brilliant guy who's all ticked off about a promotion he didn't get or an honor he didn't receive? You know the kind: gifted but miserable who shows up at a holiday faculty banquet in a cheap blue tux with a semi-automatic handgun he's nicknamed "Nancy." This planet is lousy with 'em. But here's a secret—any of those punks would, in a heartbeat, jump at the opportunity for a sparkling social life and a sense of belonging. You can never underestimate the value of friends and family. In the end, all those smarts won't buy you a pitcher with your peeps. See where we're going?

Perspective is everything and I'm going to dole out a little right now. I want you to start thinking about the Transition or, if you prefer, your *transformation*, like this: you're about to make dozens of outstanding new friends, and a significant number of them will quickly become like family to you. You'll be surrounded by amigos with whom you'll have a good deal in common. Consider all the incredible activities you'll take part in together: long, sluggish walks along the wooded trails outside of your plush Shores abode; dining on delivered cuisine

---

7. If you enjoy being mounted on a rack.

(more on that later); easy-to-grasp card games; generous helpings of the Hallmark Channel *and* Scarlet TV™; weekly motor-skills refresher courses; intramural staggering competitions; and so much more. If you don't believe me, take a gander at the vast number of leisure activities available in Chapter 5!

## FUN WITH WORDS!

Several years ago, I started encouraging everyone I dealt with— from the federal level on down—to stop using the word *zombie* and, instead, to employ the term *post-lifer*™. I was determined to eliminate negative word associations that certain uninformed people maintain regarding your current condition. *Post-lifer* has a warmer, fuzzier feel to it, and I believe it dislodges large chunks of that historical plaque of stereotyping the living dead. The Horde are zombies; you, my friend, will become something entirely unique. Doesn't "Hey, check out those post-lifers!" sound a lot less threatening than "Look out for that slimy pack of disgusting zombies!"? By using positive language, we can change our perceptions.

Here's a great example of the power of language: *Dead* is such an ugly word. A real downer.[8] Why would we ever want to use it when *post-living* works so seamlessly in its place and sounds way perkier?

---

8. Eskimos have thirty-seven different words for *dead* and all of them are equally depressing.

## POST-LIFE: THE GREAT EQUALIZER!

I believe it was Aristotle who wrote, "The worst form of inequality is to try to make unequal things equal." Well, I'm no highfalutin philosopher, but I *do* think Aristotle was a hoser for espousing such nonsense. If *he'd* ever had an opportunity to experience the post-life, I believe he would've recognized how wrong he was. Of course, this assumes he would've been capable of thinking in such a state that, logic dictates, may not have been likely. (Gosh, philosophy hurts.)

The fact is, the post-life is all about making the unequal equal; sadly (for Aristotle, that is), there's no inequality in that concept whatsoever. This is why the post-life is often referred to as "The Great Equalizer." What does that mean? Simply put, The Great Equalizer refers to the fact that whoever you were or whatever you did before doesn't matter in the post-life. Here, everyone is finally created equal. For example, let's say you were a powerful and successful CEO in your former life—now you're just one of the gang. Or maybe you were a soccer or hockey mom who taught Sunday school at your nearby Lutheran church or hunted wolves from planes. Your former reality is gone as you become another semi-remarkable citizen of the post-life. You say you were a fat kid who always got bullied? You're now a beloved skinny member of the community with scads of pals to call your own. A successful recording artist/hot model? Not anymore, but you will enjoy Soft Food Day at Cafe Patella™ in the nearby food court. The potential to be equal has infinite possibilities.

The implications of your brand-new equality will be dramatic. Any shallow concerns you once had regarding other people will vanish, too. For instance:

- *No more racism.* As was stated before, you won't give a whit whether your friends are black, white, yellow, red, or plaid. Color will no longer matter. Because of this, segregation will disappear; the bigot and the day laborer will now coexist in complete harmony. At least outside of Home Depot.

- *Not nearly as material.* John Lennon imagined a world with no possessions—be careful whatcha wish for! You won't be needing many "things" anymore, and that'll make your post-life a whole lot simpler. I bet Lennon never imagined a life this easy.

- *No more language barriers.* In the same manner that the racial divide will be bridged, so too will issues regarding foreign languages. Communication and translation problems will be a thing of the past when post-lifers are reduced to mostly speaking universal gibberish. Drivel is the new Esperanto!

- *No more social climbing.* Those dumbass worries you had about not making enough money, driving the right car, or owning that enormo mansion will be kaput. In the serenity of your ritzy, one-room apartment at the Shores, you'll find a sense of satisfaction you never thought possible.

- *No more political squabbles.* Remember how in the early twenty-first century everyone became so polarized by their political beliefs that a decent civil discourse couldn't take place? In the post-life, political debate is obsolete. Since you'll no longer be voting, you'll be even *more* apathetic about elections! Republican, Democrat, Whig, Anti-Mason—who cares? It will be understood that such affiliations are merely surface issues and surely not as important as the Thursday Night Special at Cap'n Ash's™. (See Chapter 4.)

You've just been handed five solid examples of The Great Equalizer. Naturally, religion is a biggie, too, but hold on to your horses—we've got an entire chapter coming up that's devoted to spiritual matters. Holy Moly!

## WHO LIKES DICTION?

Now that you have a clearer idea of what's in your immediate future, it's time to start laying the groundwork. Here, then, are a few exercises to sharpen vital parts of your mind. These exercises are to be practiced for an hour a day (or until the book falls out of your hands, drenched in sweat).

Let's begin with diction. Diction is an extremely important part of your training; it will help you retain your verbal skills as well as control your saliva. If another person can't understand you or is repulsed by your endless strings of drool, it will be frustrating for you and, no doubt, delay your social advancement. Such personal aggravation leads to biting and wailing, and nobody wants that.

What follows are ten key phrases that should keep your diction up to snuff. (Who said "snuff"?) Practice these phrases out loud whenever you've got downtime, which, to be blunt, should be often. Mumbling these phrases in a feverish fit will not cut it. Please compose yourself, focus, and give these a shot.

Scientists tell us that these tongue twisters assist us on many fronts. The alliterative nature of the phrases, coupled with the embedded positive messages, actually establish a "placeholder" in the mind that keeps certain faculties more intact while providing a rosier outlook. So don't let your pride get in the way of your progress. Step up to that mirror and enunciate!

1.  *Today can't be Tuesday; we have tripe on Tuesday.*

2.  *Vinny was vein-y and Valerie, too. They veered in their Volvo to steer clear of you.*

3.  *I invariably find that, most of the time, I have most of my mind.*

4.  *Kenny had kidneys and Kate had a kitten, but Mike tried to bite an old man wearing mittens.*

5.  *We're artists, we're lovers, we're not like the others.*

6.  *Jimmy had Jujubes and Tammie had a Twizzler. They found Norman on his knees, chewing on his sister.*

7.  *Gizzards and livers and lungs, oh my!*

8.  *Bobby doesn't bother with the bones. Benjy has a body of his own.*

9.  *Some stumble, some stagger, I triumph, I swagger.*

10. *Two tiny toes and a hobo's nose made a real nice treat for Sarah Rose.*

Fun, aren't they? Work on wringing out the emotion in each phrase. Deliver each one with authority and élan. I strongly suggest working in front of a mirror at first; you'll be able to watch yourself and not fall into any unsavory patterns such as slurring or growling. And know this: I'm a realist. When the mirror is no longer your best buddy (usually within about thirty to thirty-six hours), it's okay to practice without it.

## OH, BOY—A MULTIPLE CHOICE TEST!

Now let's try a different test. Don't be put off by the following set of questions; they'll seem absurdly simple at first. Mark my words, though: in a matter of days, you'll struggle with this same test, but you also will have benefited from having just taken it. In other words, your memory *will* retain bits of information and, at this stage, *anything* that gets retained is considered a major coup.

Let's begin.

1. How many letters are in the alphabet?
   a. 28
   b. 26
   c. Arggggghhhhh
   d. Skull cap

2. How many even numbers are there between 1 and 10?
   a. 3
   b. Fibula
   c. 5
   d. Stooopid numbrz

3. Chuck found some change in his pocket: five dimes, two nickels, and a shimmering new penny. How much money did Chuck end up having?

a. 61 cents

b. Hungry now

c. Would like to sink teeth into Chuck's shoulder

d. 62 cents

4. Name the Great Lakes.

a. Erie, Michigan, Ssssssssssss, Kill!

b. Erie, Michigan, Superior, Only want to forage

c. Erie, Michigan, Superior, Ontario, Have to eat soon

d. Erie, Michigan, Superior, Ontario, Huron

5. Define *verb*.

a. A word that means stuff about doing stuff.

b. A word that denotes action—like biting.

c. A word that denotes an action, an occurrence, or a state of being.

d. Ears are tasty!

6. What is the Golden Rule?

a. Die, human!

b. Grrrrrrrrrrrrrrrrrrrrrrrr

c. Eat first, ask later.

d. Do unto others as you would have them do unto you.

7. Who was America's first president?

a. Settler Bob of the *Mayflower*

b. John Adams

c. George Washington

d. Forearm kind of chewy

8. Raul, your zombie friend, is taking a stroll to the Dark Corridor. It's 12 miles away from where he started, and on his first day he got halfway there. How far did he travel?

a. I go with him—food there.

b. 12 miles

c. Is too 12 miles! Uhhhhh, head hurt now.

d. 6 miles

9. What planet are you from?

a. Blue

b. Green

c. Earth

d. Die

10. How many sides are there in a square?

a. Don't care.

b. Care even less since answer a.

c. Stil not karing—wunder how test wud taste…

d. 4

As you have just experienced, this test offers you the "before and after" ability to see how your symptoms are progressing. Within each group of answers is the right answer, but as the Transition proceeds, other answers will start making more sense to you. To prove this, retake the test in several hours, and don't be surprised if several of your responses are different and at some point you attempt to bite the test. Don't blame yourself. As the Virus spreads, you'll become, shall we say, more single-minded. The answer that may have once appeared droll or silly now will be the one you'll choose.

# TIME TO CIRCLE THINGS!

The last exercise is a short one; it's more conceptual in nature, so don't get testy. It'll help preserve the higher functions of the mind that are primarily used for math and metal shop.

In the following groups, choose which of the illustrated items is not the same as the others and circle it.

A.

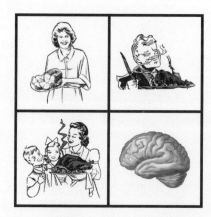

B.

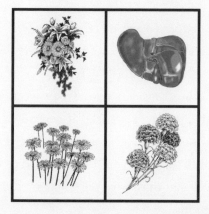

C.

D.

E.

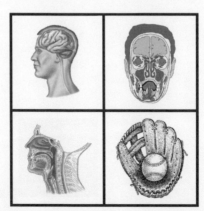

I can't repeat this enough: by regularly taking these seemingly simple tests that target specific parts of your intellect, you'll notice long-term results that will help keep your QScale number up and make you more socially acceptable. It will behoove you to review these tests every few hours for as long as you're capable of doing so.

## TIME FOR A NEW HABIT OR TWO!

So now that your mind is sharper and less cluttered and you're at the top of your game (I exaggerate for emphasis), let's hook you up with additional social and personal guidance. Strap yourself in for Chapter 2, because you're about to go from feverish to *fabulous*!

# THE 14 HABITS OF HIGHLY EFFECTIVE ZOMBIES:

## ETIQUETTE AND BEHAVIOR

A major event has occurred that will significantly impact every aspect of your life, including your involuntary functions. That, however, is no reason to come unglued. This is the moment when you must dig your deepest for strength and dignity. It's time to gain perspective about where you've been and where you're headed. Now is when you must learn how to become *highly effective*. Not to be confused with "infected" or, for that matter, "affected." The world doesn't need any more poseurs.

Let's say you were invited to a swanky soirée. You wouldn't want to show up and behave like a heathen, now, would you? Of course not—you'd choose to be that same slick operator you've always been. Indeed, you want to exude the requisite dignity (there's that word again), grace, and charm to make everyone gaga at the gala.

While the following chapters will address *external* issues such as hygiene, grooming, and diet, *this* chapter will focus on bettering your internal self. And we'll readdress internal needs later in the book, but for now it's important to pour the foundation of self-esteem (but beware the rebar—it's poke-y). And by introducing you to the 14 Habits™ while you're still able to grok a concept or two, you're virtually ensured that they'll stay with you. (Well, at least the first seven.)

Yes, the 14 Habits, as you will soon see, are a valuable device that serves to help you smooth out your increasingly "rough edges." The following chart is designed to illustrate the differences between someone such as *you* (after completing the coursework regarding the Habits) and the Horde (who, by choosing to ignore the Habits, are seemingly incapable of bettering themselves). Observe how dramatic these differences are.

| SCENARIO | POST-LIFE WITHOUT 14 HABITS | POST-LIFE WITH 14 HABITS |
|---|---|---|
| Motorist stranded along roadside at night in need of assistance with flat tire. | Creep up on car, head-butt window until smashed, pull human from car, bite skull. | Assist motorist with flat tire and admire cranium while making small talk (very small). Refuse offer for payment. |
| Girl Scouts knock on front door selling cookies. | Grab smallest human, bite skull. | Purchase a box or two of Thin Mints and politely inquire as to why there aren't any more of those delicious Medulla deLites that were offered last year. Don't scowl. |

| SCENARIO | POST-LIFE WITHOUT 14 HABITS | POST-LIFE WITH 14 HABITS |
|---|---|---|
| Pair of teenage sweethearts parked in Lover's Lane, making out. | Bite human male first. Female slower; Horde friends descend on her down the road. | While you're out for a stroll, wish the kids a pleasant evening. Resist urge to smell their heads. |
| Large gathering for memorial service at local cemetery. | Recall that the word *buffet* might describe this scenario. | Respectfully keep your distance and allow the mourners their moment. Offer condolences if and when appropriate. Control drool. |
| Mall in lockdown; shoppers terrified and in near-riot. | Like biting fish in barrel. | Stay calm. Compulsions increasingly hard to control. Excuse yourself to dressing room of department store for possible light lunch-meat snack and irrepressible moaning. |
| Honeymoon couple's vehicle stuck in mud outside of cemetery during thunderstorm; bride has twisted her ankle, her dress is torn, and groom needs his insulin. | What could be easier? Similar to canned hunt with former Veep. | Gather friends and help move vehicle. Sniff car seats. Fondle damaged ankle if possible. Score insulin for puny male. Later, lick syringe. |

## WHO THUNK THIS STUFF UP?

The 14 Habits were first introduced in two separate books, written by the same author, who chose to remain anonymous. Allegedly, said author was a well-meaning psychologist who dashed off the first book, *The 7 Habits*, at the request of our government; at that time, the Feds were seeking a strong set of behavioral guidelines to impart to the infected and to certain citizens of Boulder, Colorado. Subsequently, federal workers attempted to teach these habits to Horde members, an assignment that went badly from the get-go. Multiple workers were lost within minutes.[9]

Once the Feds abandoned the Horde and figured out who the optimal recipients of this advice would be, the book proved to be an enormous success. It wasn't long before the author was encouraged to write another. Sadly, in celebrating his literary success, he developed quite the addiction problem, and *Okay, Here Are 7 More Habits* was not as popular, valuable, or cogent as the first. Frankly, it sucked. Please keep this in mind as you review the entire list.

## NOW MORE THAN EVER—SOCIAL GRACES

Here's a term that may make you laugh: "a proper zombie." Sounds goofy, doesn't it? But that's one way of looking at who a post-lifer is—a proper zombie. It's true that you *will* have a few physical qualities in common with those in the Horde, but for the most part it's your *behavior* and *character* that will set you apart. And snappier threads.

Ultimately, that's what the Habits develop—stronger character. Some of the 14 Habits address etiquette; others concern the most productive ways to manage your post-life; and at the end of the list, the Habits become downright dopey. (Those are the "7 More" discussed earlier.)

---

9. The Boulder populace wasn't so receptive, either.

I've intentionally kept the descriptions brief so that you'll have a shot at retaining as much as possible. By distilling the info into simple catchphrases, your recall will be maximized. Another example of neuroplasticity in action!

## HABIT #1: TABLE MANNERS

Eating with your hands is never acceptable. You weren't born in a barn. Sure, you may see a lot of your brethren and sistren behaving coarsely while dining alfresco, but you need to ignore them, because that's not how you roll. (Remember, just because everyone in the Horde does it doesn't make it right.)

Civilization is crumbling but *you're* staying civilized. So, please, always use utensils. Rather than tearing your dinner apart and gnawing on it, make the effort to pick up a knife and fork and cut your food correctly. Really, it's not that much work. Alas, if you *absolutely must* descend on a poor random creature with your friends, keep a spork or other easily tucked-away utensil on your person for such regrettable "manner emergencies." For that matter, also keep a wet wipe or two handy.

Be advised, as a result of the Disaster, there's a condition from which your former fellow humans suffer called "zolimia." Unlike bulimia, this is an affliction where the amount and nature of what you eat makes certain humans heave. If you're constantly gnashing and slashing like a crazed animal, it will make some folks ill and, over time, no one will want to associate with you. Please be sensitive to the plight of zolimics and dial it down a notch or twelve.

Think manners don't matter? Think again. A recent government report found that the refined post-lifers are more likely to get into the most exclusive Scarlet Shores facilities. Additionally, they are a whopping *ninety-three percent* more well-adjusted once they arrive. No question that good manners are a great investment in your future!

And what of the aforementioned alfresco concept? Social graces dictate that you accept your meals inside, around a table, sans snarling. Believe me, no human has a problem with a polite patio gathering at the Shores or a lighthearted picnic on the lawn now and again. But the idea that it is somehow acceptable to be out wandering around at all hours, chewing on the first living thing you come across, is simply wrong and bad form.

How to put this best? No roadkill (unless you're out maggot-gathering—see Chapter 3). Roadkill = really bad form. You didn't behave in such a manner when you were living, and you won't be acting like that in the post-life, either.

## HABIT #2: "PLEASE" AND "THANK YOU"

To my mind, Habit #2 sets its sights on one of the most disturbing traits of typical Horde conduct: entirely too much uncouth grunting and grabbing. While it is true your vocabulary will shrink to that of a first grader (if you're lucky), the plucky pair of "please" and "thank you" can still play an effective role in your everyday speech. And they're *not* that hard to remember.

For example, let's say you encounter a situation where several Horde-ish folks are having a light roadside snack. You were just told not to participate in such behavior, but you know how you get. So if you are joining your comrades, instead of elbowing your way in to snatch an available limb or organ, utilize "please" and "thank you" in order to ask for what you want. By doing so, a small slice of civilization is preserved. It's the little things that keep us human. Some of us.

What follows are examples of sample dialogue. Read each one aloud and make a point to emphasize every "please" and "thank you":

1. "Can I please have that thigh?"
2. "Pass the ribs, please."
3. "Thank you for the pancreas, Danny. It was delicious."
4. "Excuse me, ma'am—may we please bite your face?"
5. "Mindy, I never properly thanked you for that nice brain platter you put together for our function the other day. How very kind of you."
6. "Please stop screaming. We get hungry when we walk. Thanks!"

What a difference "please" and "thank you" make! They promote civility, kindness, and respect—three more words that will become even more important in the days and weeks to come.

## HABIT #3: YOU'RE STILL GENTLEMEN AND LADIES

I have long believed that the social graces are what separate mankind from the rest of the animal kingdom. For example, bonobo chimps are known for being abysmal houseguests, and you absolutely can't get a ferret to return a phone call. Likewise, within days of the completed

Transition, if left to your own devices, you too will likely "forget" everyday niceties, especially proper behavior vis-à-vis the opposite sex. If *that's* the loutish lifestyle you desire, you might as well stop reading now and go live with the bonobos.

The following particulars may seem antiquated or non-PC, but so be it. We are looking to maintain a certain standard here, a sense of chivalry, if you will. So if you're a man, you will continue to open doors for the fairer sex, pull out her chair, and, when accompanying her down a street, shamble on the outside lane. And if you're a woman, you will continue to curtsy (bending slowly), cross your legs politely, and properly hold out your pinkie finger when sipping tea or whatever macabre fluids you might end up consuming. In order to have the best post-life possible, your public conduct toward the opposite sex (or the gender of your choice) needs to be impeccable. What you choose to do behind closed doors will be your own disgusting business.

## HABIT #4: SHHHHH—OTHERS LIVE HERE, TOO!

One of the essential tenets of proper decorum is to avoid disturbing others with unnecessary noise. Being a member of your own "rad crew" of post-lifers does not exempt you from old-fashioned courtesy. You are expected to embrace this Habit, use your behavioral adjustment skills (see one of the next sections re: your temper), and apply common sense in order to know the appropriate times to raise a ruckus. I understand that you and your pals are an extremely exuberant bunch, filled with a certain *joie de morte*. Indeed, enthusiasm is not to be discouraged. However, if you want to be respected as you evolve, you must respect others. An important aspect of this respect is paying attention to others' boundaries, especially their right to enjoy peace and quiet without your incessant yelping and lip smacking. Remember, bucko: no growling in the grocery store, no snarling at Starbucks, no mewling at moviegoers. If you *do* feel the need to express yourself in an unsavory manner, find a private place in which to act out—e.g., a gas station rest room, a storm cellar, or the freezer of an abandoned cafe.

## HABIT #5: PUNCTUALITY

As the state of catatonia inches ever closer, your autonomic nervous system responses will begin to lag a bit. (And by "a bit," I mean a lot.) Because you'll be moving more slowly, it's going to take you much longer to do *everything*. For example, when you make lunch, plan on completing your cooking closer to dinner. Consequently, you'll want to start prepping for lunch at dawn. Point being, it's important that you begin to factor this sluggishness into your datebook. Plan ahead with what's left of your head.

An illustration: you've got an appointment for your annual government stamp review at the Department of Social Services on Tuesday at 3:00 p.m. Back in your days as a human, you could head out around 2:40 and make that meeting with minutes to spare. Since you'll no longer be driving, you'll need to factor in a reasonable amount of time to either (a) take a ShuffleCraft or (b) stagger over at a blistering 2 miles per hour in order to arrive at the appointed hour. Perhaps www.saunterquest.com can help you plan the best route, or maybe you should seek out the guidance of one who's "walked" to the Department of Social Services before—preferably, a friend who continues to have a memory cell or two.[10] Remember, no one likes a "Tardy Tommy." With a modest amount of preparation, you can continue to be the "Timely Timmy" you've always been.

---

10. Lotsa luck.

## HABIT #6: ANGER MANAGEMENT

After years of testing and polling, scientists are still unclear as to why, exactly, the Horde is so darn torqued. Some believe the root of their anger is hunger; others attribute it to abandonment issues or psychological scars left over from that middle-school industrial arts class. Perhaps we'll never know. Nevertheless, I can assure you that you're going to be the picture of calm, because you know that such public displays of rage (PDRs) are distasteful (unless you've been subjected to a Matthew McConaughey movie, and then no one will blame you).

Meanwhile, whenever you start to feel the blood lust rising or maniacal thinking begins to screw with your psyche, try this exercise: sit quietly and, with eyes closed, find that "special place" where you feel relaxed, tranquil, and loved. Maybe it's the memory of that astounding cake you had at your ninth birthday party, Tommy Frazier's crushing 75-yard touchdown run in the Fiesta Bowl, your vacation in Maui (save for the poi), the twelve-page poem a boy wrote for you in sixth grade, Jack Kirby's Galactus, or your first session of heavy petting in the backseat of that Gremlin. Whatever your "special place" is—be it person, place, or thing—visualize it and then focus on it intently. Notice how quickly you become composed and calm, especially if you're still in the backseat of the Gremlin.

The previous exercise is actually a form of meditation.[11] Now let's apply techniques that more closely resemble biofeedback. For those of you who might not remember the '70s (and few do), biofeedback is an interactive form of alternative medicine whereby patients attempt to regulate their emotional states and bodily functions through increased concentration, awareness, and aluminum foil—kind

---

11. For more commentary on meditation and specific exercises that can be implemented on a daily basis, please see Chapter 11. That'll set your shit straight!

of like how I learned to control myself and not go for the gun whenever *Maury* comes on. For our purposes here, however, we're going to give this exercise a more accurate name: Necrofeedback™.[12] Like its "bio" cousin, Necrofeedback is a method by which you're able to adjust some of your missing physical functions. By concentrating on your "special place" and by experiencing an elevated level of relaxation, you'll notice a slowing of your involuntary processes, even if they're mostly absent. For example, if you're lucky enough to still have a pulse, observe how it slows down even more during this practice. And while an unavoidable few of you may have stopped breathing, there will be a discernible difference in how short and shallow your non-breath becomes.

No question that Necrofeedback is an invaluable way to rein in your nasty temper as well as being a nifty tool to be used at the appropriate time—i.e., the bulk of your waking hours. By learning to control your fury and thereby suppress the lust to feast on a frightened stranger, you'll end up being more accepted in society and, in general, more well liked at your given Shores facility.

## HABIT #7: GOOD-TO-MIDDLING SELF-ESTEEM

Everything we've gone over thus far won't be worth its weight in gizzards if an upbeat self-image isn't developed over time. Being kind to yourself and feeling good *about* yourself is imperative. You cannot become self-punishing in any way. It's not your fault you were bitten. It's not your doing that the Transition has begun. Embrace this kernel of wisdom now: life was always about change, and the post-life won't be any different.

---

12. Necrofeedback ©2009 David P. Murphy, all rights reserved.

In order to move forward with this course work and accept what lies on the other side of the Transition, you need a sunny outlook and a boatload of poise. It's time to remember the great person you always were and the positive actions you consistently took on behalf of others (assuming you weren't a loudmouthed radio personality with an OxyContin addiction). In moments of despair, center yourself with the aforementioned Necrofeedback practice and do *not* indulge your compulsions. Giving in to such feelings and behavior will throw you off course and will only lead to "barbeques" around car fires. Impromptu parties might feel good in the moment, but eventually revulsion will rear its ugly head.

If your self-esteem was lacking in your former life, consider your current condition to be the tabula rasa you deserve—a blank slate and a cold (and sweaty) reboot. You will shed the old skin of existence (so to speak) and be reborn (sort of). All those lingering issues of yours will be wiped away with your impending downgrade. That chronic fear of Mary Hart and/or spiders? No more. The incident in study hall when that creepy teacher's aide longingly leered at you from across the room? History! That irrational anxiety you experience regarding Andre Rieu and Esteban? Be gone!

Think of all the money you'll save on therapy. Yes, the silver lining here is humungous—there won't be enough RAM upstairs to keep your emotional crud in storage.

To complement that fact, there's additional, related news on the medical front. In a landmark study published in the *New Jersey Journal of Medicine*, the true miracle that is neuroplasticity is revealed. Apparently, when an injury or infection to the brain occurs, the essential information of our lives as well as *the information most recently acquired* is what the brain first attempts to preserve and remap. In your case, this suggests the good rises to the top. All the torturous memories and ideas about our past that have haunted us end up being attended to only *after* all recent, vital positive data has been preserved. Consequently, the vast majority of the crummy stuff that served to drain our energy ends up on the cutting-room floor, deleted due to a lack of remaining resources. It's almost as if the brain is Windows-based! The blue screen of post-life!

## BECAUSE SEQUELS ARE NEVER AS GOOD

We've arrived at the *7 More Habits*, which are usually referred to as the "lesser habits." Given that the author was out of his gourd while writing the sequel, these seven are included out of deference. I have taken the liberty of adding editorial remarks to guide you swiftly through these dunderheaded concepts. How much interest you devote to them is entirely up to you.

- Habit #8: *Obedience*. Strange one to begin a second book with. Not a bad trait, but not so important unless, perhaps, you're a collie or a submissive.

- Habit #9: *Moderation*. Methinks the author was talking to himself here. The inner addict was starting to make his presence felt.

- Habit #10: *Boxed Wine*. Ruh-roh.

- Habit #11: *Ability to Pull Coins from Ears of Strangers*. Not sure where he was going with this one; kind of a sharp bat-turn. But, hey, let's give him the benefit of the doubt. I mean, who doesn't love that damn coin trick?

- Habit #12: *Huffing*. Okay, so did anyone even *proof* this second book? Disgusting.

- Habit #13: *Ability to Sell Everything for Whatever I Can Get*. Certainly not a habit and a completely unappealing personal trait. The writer appears to have a geranium in his cranium by now.

- Habit #14: *Meth*. Bingo! The devil appears. It was rumored that upon completion of the second book, the author spent several months at Betty Ford mumbling and recuperating. Old habits die hard.

## MOVING ON

As a result of implementing the 14 Habits (or at least the first seven), your mind will, technically speaking, give these habits "cuts" at the front of the brain line. As with the diction test, by having practiced these regularly, you'll be better positioned to succeed in the post-life. And in the big picture, you'll feel oodles better about yourself. Got that? Oodles.

Now it's time for a little reward: the latest cutting-edge information regarding which medicines might be right for you. A lot of pharma companies are damn anxious to hear what you think of their wares, so let's not keep 'em waiting.

# THE COURAGE TO MEDICATE:
## YOUR PHARMACEUTICAL OPTIONS

If, while reading this book, you started taking commercial pain medications to take the edge off, I apologize. I probably should've mentioned this sooner: none of the over-the-counter stuff helps. Like pea shooters on a whale hunt, these pills, patches, and silly salves stand no chance of taking down the bogie. For serious relief, you need the stuff that's *behind* the counter. *Wayyy* behind the counter.

Let's reflect on your situation: it's not easy when you first realize you have a problem. You spend precious time in denial, avoiding the issues that need to be addressed. Sure, in your screwed-up state you could probably snag a gig on a reality show, but what's that going to get you?[13] You can't continue to live your life suffering—it's completely unnecessary. And the answer is *not* about numbing your physical and emotional pain levels with Kountry Kwencher or QualiTussin. Such products are nothing more than namby-pamby stuff any wily nine-year-old could pilfer at a Piggly Wiggly. You need nothing less than world-class meds.

---

13. Besides Tila Tequila.

## SO MUCH FOR CLEAN LIVING

Now is not the time to worry about any potential addiction issues. In fact, your problem is a lack of *suitable* addictions. You need to get a quality monkey or two on your back and pronto!

Indeed, swift action is crucial here. You no longer have the luxury of waiting to see if your spirits lift before you call that HMO psychotherapist whom your Human Resources person recommended. Similarly, you've got no time to track down that supposedly holistic guy your friend's friend knows who can squeeze you in next week and, after a four-minute meeting/reading, will hand you a packet of herbs that smells like turds and cinnamon. And that sweat lodge weekend you've been considering ain't gonna make a dent either, so save your beads and pelts, kimosabe.

No, right now you need the real deal—the full-tilt boogie, mind-shattering, prescription-strength shit in Judy Garland–sized doses. So because *Z4Z* loves it some clients, here's where you receive the first of several perks, and they're coming to you simply because *you bought this book*!

## SCANNED AND BEAUTIFUL

Surely you noticed when you purchased this book that just after the UPC code was scanned, you were, too. Hope you didn't freak. That scan was a type of tech that allowed your newly altered bioinfo (usually about 9.8 terabytes) to be downloaded and added to a cutting-edge database housed in a subterranean fortress in the mountains of Wyoming. This database holds the bioinfo for hundreds of thousands of folks such as you, who are all active parts of a grand experiment in healing and marketing.

By obtaining your bioinfo directly, different high-profile vendors have been alerted and have *already sent you* exclusive products and offers, each designed to assist you in any number of relevant ways. You'll be pleased to know that four of those vendors are major pharmaceutical companies! Plus, once you've been scanned, we can cut out that pesky middleman, otherwise known as your doctor. You heard right: with the "auto-initiate" feature of these particular drugs, if you so choose, your entire Transition can be doctor-free. No more white coat syndrome for you.

Hold it. You're worried about not having a personal physician available during this time? Well, you know the old adage: if you want to stay healthy, stay away from the doctor. This is especially true post-Disaster. You do *not* need to be exposed to any other infections. And how much good has your medical coverage ever done you? The Disaster Kare Kiosks™ on every corner are overwhelmed, and their service is marginal at best. Besides, the *Z4Z* program, including its set of complimentary trial offers, has now been endorsed by the NMA (National Medical Association™)[14] as a "sufficiently adequate

By the way, if you happen to be one of those slimy folks who isn't infected but bought the book because you heard you could get a bunch of free drugs, sorry to burst your codependent bubble, but your bioinfo scan at the point of purchase showed no P.V. activity. Those cashiers weren't born yesterday. Accordingly, nothing will be arriving at your door, so quit trying to put one over on the system. We're on to you, Bub.

---

14. Not associated with the AMA.

outpatient solution for dealing with the tragic effects of the Provo Virus."
The NMA calls 'em like they sees 'em.

## I WANT A NEW DRUG!

A dark gray box marked "Urgent and Confidential" will soon be delivered
to you at your current address. This is your CareBox™. Inside, you'll
find several samples of various prescription drugs along with a number of
other items, which we'll enumerate later. I urge you to read the directions
that accompany each of the drugs and decide which of them *you think* will
be best for you. It would be ideal if you could get an expert's opinion before
you take the medication, but we're on a tight deadline here.

In order to jump-start this process, what follows are brief descriptions
of the drugs, accompanied by a bit of info regarding each one's efficacy
and suitability.

### ROMERIN®

This powerful, red, heart-shaped pill has recently emerged from its final
round of clinical trials and is now available for both the general public
and post-lifers. The FDA and QualiCorps are equally ecstatic with this
drug, so if you're going to medicate yourself (and why wouldn't you?), it
should be considered a serious candidate.

Here's why: upon entering the Transition, over two-thirds of those who
took Romerin were able to preserve, on average, an impressive twenty-
two percent more of their motor skills and ability to be rational than those
who took only the placebo. On the aforementioned QScale, this puts the
Romerin patients' level of humanity solidly in the neighborhood of, say,
Tony Little. (By the way, I don't recall "America's Personal Trainer" ever
being offered as a choice during my high school "Career Days.")

Romerin works its magic by inhibiting those nasty bastards—the excitotoxic amino acids (particularly N-methyl-D-aspartate, for anyone keeping score at home)—thereby helping to hold together your noggin's neural net. What the h-e-double-hockey-sticks does that mean, you ask? Only that Romerin will allow your brain to hang in there long enough for neuroplasticity to properly do the voodoo it do.

Obviously, no drug is one hundred percent safe, and there's simply not time to detail the full complement of Romerin's side effects. Nevertheless, you should know that a longing for library paste and a need to be flogged at a Hardee's are the two least desirable complications. There are also the standard side effects such as stroke, loss of hearing, or fear of weasels. Food interaction warning: no Funions or Grape Fanta during the first two weeks.

## PRODUCTIVA®

This medicine has been on the market since the late 1950s. Originally used to treat Jumping Frenchman Disorder in Maine lumberjacks, this diminutive orange, axe-shaped pill has recently found a significantly more modern role in helping the recently bitten. Its popularity is mainly attributed to the prodigious amounts of energy it produces, most likely due to its low-dose Ritalin "frosting." Productiva could enable you to one day get off the floor or even out of a chair. QScale effectiveness has yet to be fully determined; nevertheless, preliminary studies indicate you most likely won't get the generous "humanity bump" that Romerin provides, but, golly, you'll get a lot more accomplished.

In addition to the side effects of dry mouth, a proclivity toward gambling, and a penchant for fawning over croquet mallets, Productiva can be highly addictive, so please do not stop taking this medication without the help of a certified professional or lumberjack. (Maine residency not required.) If you do not properly wean yourself off Productiva, withdrawal pains can be severe enough to produce world-class gurning. Food interaction warning: pickled eggs and pudding can't be combined while taking this drug.

## BLISSIUM®

Here we have a mellow herbal product that hails from a spunky Native American–owned company located in what's left of New Mexico. Derived from traditional natural ingredients, Blissium assists the healing process by inducing a deep state of relaxation in the individual. This bright yellow pill has a patented formula that includes chamomile, THC, and peyote extract along with a form of Datura, the notorious Caribbean herb known to cause delirium. While not technically a pharmaceutical product, Blissium is mentioned here due to the success rate it has enjoyed in reducing pain, boosting appetites, and increasing the frequency of staring at the toaster oven. With Blissium, QScale effectiveness is negligible, but, honestly, you probably won't give a damn. Food interaction warning: no Circus Peanuts for the first forty-eight hours.

## CEREBELLA®

This is a late entry from a British manufacturer that offers up a novel strategy. Through the magic of DNA tinkering and New Age gibberish, the Brits have found a way to unlock what they call "the Confidence Gene." In a bulky blue capsule with its unmistakable red exclamation point, CereBella produces a cool, assured demeanor, providing patients with an incredible lift in self-esteem and the ability to yammer on about themselves for hours at a time, not unlike a lobotomized Trump.

CereBella accomplishes its mission by including a stiff hit of naltrexone in its patented formula. This ingredient blocks the theopioid/endorphin pathways and is normally used to reduce addictive behavior (e.g., to heroin or zBay[15]). By greatly impairing the need for, oh, say, "flesh," the patient experiences an overwhelming sense of inflated self-worth, which aids in masking a good deal of the pain associated with the Transition. (The drugs giveth and the drugs taketh away.) With the proper dosage, QScale effectiveness could put you at the level of a persistently salivating Flavor Flav. Food interaction warning: none.

## WHAT THE HECK ELSE IS IN THAT DADGUM CAREBOX?

In addition to the sample packs of each drug, the box will contain an impressive number of products and offers from various vendors. If anything from the subsequent list appears to be missing, please report the omission to 1-877-CAREBOX and your items will be promptly replaced.

---

15. Where else can you find a human kidney with a "Bite It Now" price?

## CAREBOX CHECKLIST

| | |
|---|---|
| ☐ | one (1) hot water bottle |
| ☐ | one (1) package of sidewalk chalk |
| ☐ | two (2) joy buzzers |
| ☐ | seven (7) Hungry Boy MeatMasks™ |
| ☐ | one (1) tin of smelt in hot sauce |
| ☐ | nine (9) bottles of HammerMe Pain Negotiator™ sleep aid |
| ☐ | one (1) deck of tarot cards |
| ☐ | one (1) 12 oz. chocolate bar |
| ☐ | four (4) rubber mallets |
| ☐ | one (1) bottle of Ear-igate |
| ☐ | three (3) bags of L'il Smokies |
| ☐ | one (1) Slinky |
| ☐ | one (1) coupon good for a free car wash at any of the 253 Dr. Soapee's Auto-terias™. Dr. Soapee says: "Wash your car—while you still can!" |

Please note: the use of the items in the box will become more obvious as we proceed deeper into the book. Along with the drugs and these additional goods, your CareBox should get you over the hump of the Transition.

Again, only you will know which one of these pills will be the best fit for you, so proceed slowly. Don't just start popping those puppies like a Dr. Drew patient. Give the provided documentation a more than cursory look. And by no means should you combine certain of these meds with one another. For example, Romerin mixed with CereBella has been known to create a confident yet subhuman persona, like Glenn Beck when he's spouting one of his kooky commentaries. In addition, the resulting combo platter of Productiva mixed with Blissium produces a disturbingly motivated stoner. Who wants that?

Other than the aforementioned combinations, the sky's the limit. Mix 'n' match 'n' knock yourself out. Literally.[16]

## WHAT ABOUT WHADDYACALLIT—THAT HOMEOPATHIC STUFF?

Apart from Blissium, natural and herbal remedies have been around since day one, and in recent years there'd been quite a worldwide resurgence in their use. That was, of course, until the Disaster, which largely put homeopathic remedies out of commish. Think about it—no known drugs or antibiotics were making a freakin' difference during the first several years. The herbal approach lasted about nine nanoseconds once everyone realized that the recently bitten were suffering from something far worse than "trapped chi" or "nasal backlog." So much for that nutty neti pot!

---

16. I've grown rather fond of mixing four HammerMe's with a Grande Cadillac margarita. I sleep like a baby!

However, several other semi-natural treatments that evolved after the Disaster are now enjoying a large degree of popularity. You might find any of the following to be effective when used along with your meds.

## MAGGOT BAGS

It was already well established that a small bag of maggots, taped to a wound, could promote healing in an expedited manner. Over the last two years, the medical community has taken this idea several steps further in order to increase the maggot bag's efficacy and decrease the number of underemployed maggots. Where once the fine mesh bags were roughly the size of a child's sock, now they're more akin to pillowcases—soft, squishy pillowcases squirming in place from the wiggling of thousands of maggots.

For proper therapeutic use, place one of these bags on your chest, under your legs, or on any bodily surface that's giving you grief. Do your best to relax with the undulating bag, and you'll be amazed—abrasions heal more quickly and skin tone is marginally improved. Perhaps the niftiest aspect is that the maggot bag doesn't cost you an arm and a leg (as it were), because the ingredients are free. There's no need for you to buy the commercially produced version; you can easily make your own. Any old pillowcase will do as long as the material is especially worn and the thread count is low.

And maggots, well, I don't need to tell you how plentiful they are—the world is lousy with 'em! From collecting the critters on curbside leftovers to the wounds on your colleagues, harvesting maggots is as easy as pickin' paw-paws. Sure, the concept is nauseating, but stop spazzing out about it and instead focus on your health.

## LEECHES

Like maggots, leeches are a popular folk remedy that has been used throughout history for numerous ailments, including the vapors, rickets, and the curing of the insane. These delightful little helpers just might do you a world of good. Yes, initial exposure to leeching can indeed be disturbing, but it's nothing compared to a single listening of either "Afternoon Delight" or Il Divo. Our modern leeching experiments have brought us a fresh, out-of-the-test-tube, hopped-up, enhanced line o' leeches that are much larger and leaner than their candy-ass cousins. Apply a couple of these suckers (pun intended!) to an infected area of your body and watch those tripartite jaws work their enzyme magic. These babies can hoover the bad juju outta you quicker than you can say "Jonas Salk." And when you're done with 'em, they fry up like nobody's business. Cooking tip: get your BBQ good and hot, grill about three minutes on each side, and go easy on the salt.

## OATMEAL DUNK

Let me get personal for a moment. When I was a kid, I had impetigo, a skin infection caused by a couple of types of non-pizza-related bacteria. One of the treatments my mom used was wrapping oatmeal in a wet washcloth (I suppose no maggots were available) and dabbing the cloth on the sores. Now, flash-forward a number of years later and imagine my surprise that while doing research on behalf of this book, I discovered the oatmeal soak is back in vogue. These days, however, the cloth has been eliminated and the treatment takes place in a bathtub full of warm water mixed with two gallons of grade-A ground oats. The patient is encouraged to sit and soak for one full hour in the grainy, pasty muck, letting the oats extract all accumulated daily toxins from his or her body. And, yes, butter and brown sugar can be added to your liking.

## ELECTROPOISE

Not quite homeopathic, this seemingly innocuous machine is finding an outrageous new life with patients during and after the Transition. Considered at one time to be a quack medical contrivance, this electronic device claims to do impressive things. By turning it on and attaching its small electrodes directly to your skin, oxygen will be absorbed more rapidly into the skin, thereby possibly promoting enhanced dermal regeneration. Who knows? Maybe the device lives up to its claims. Hell, I once bought one of those crappy Kevin Trudeau books.

### WHAT ABOUT THE INDEPENDENT MEDICAL RVS I'VE SEEN?

By all means, avoid medical RVs and all the knockoffs that are out there. The IMRVs are a classic case of a handful of scumbags trying to make a few stamps on the side by offering curbside therapeutic services that are, by the way, worthless and possibly dangerous. You'll recognize these phony physicians by their converted cruisers with the luminous logos on the side. Worst of all, they're not even licensed to drive RVs. And do *not* accept any free drug samples from them. They're dealing some bad shit, man.

## IT'S STORY TIME!

I hope this chapter has alleviated your concerns regarding how to best address your medical needs. Many who enter the Transition tend to be exceedingly jumpy and fret about the future far too much. Relax. Once the CareBox arrives, your sitch will improve big-time. Let the products do their work, and if you follow the directions you've been given, you should feel in the pink in no time flat. A very pale pink.

It's time to take a moment to reflect on "who not to become." The following chapter offers the first episode of *Tales from the Horde* as a cautionary, morality tale. Although it may, at first blush, appear to be like a frivolous B-movie adaptation, dig a bit deeper and I believe you'll find this story provides the perfect illustration of how you don't want to end up—i.e., falling in with the Horde. Or in front of them.

Once you've finished reading the episode, meet me over at the Hall o' Fixins for some major eats. Make sure you bring that towering appetite of yours, if you still have one.

# INTERLUDE

## ❧ TALES FROM THE HORDE: ❧

# TERROR AT LAKE ROMNEY

Remember, friends: as you read this, pay close attention to how distasteful the Horde can be. Perhaps such a close examination will encourage you to complete the *Z4Z* program even more quickly. Wouldn't *that* be dandy...

How did we not see that coming? How did we not realize we'd entered our own, private horror story? I should've known better. It was the field trip to hell and we're lucky we're still alive.

The Regular Six (as we called ourselves), Tim and Tammy, Russ and Becky, and me and my girl, Jeannie, decided to whoop it up one Friday night because it was Tim's birthday. We were bored with our standard locations de whoop, and Russ brilliantly suggested we all go for a drive up old Highway 31, out to the edge of the local Zone, to where most of it had been cordoned off. There is, however, an area adjacent to Lake Romney where you can squeeze through the barricades in a smaller vehicle and soak up some moonlight on water. At the time it sounded like a swell idea, so we packed up our coolers, blankets, and lanterns, crammed into my car, and headed out.

I hadn't set foot on Romney Beach for about a year and, to my surprise, found it in an even greater state of disrepair than what was rumored. The pavilion was gutted, the picnic tables stolen, and the FortiFence on the perimeter of the Zone had softball-sized holes in it, apparently from that freakish hailstorm we had last year. The Feds had assured our community they'd send out a team of repair guys and have the Fence patched up, but that hadn't happened yet. There were plans to repopulate the occasional watchtower, too, but I guess the funding ran out. The economy went to hell after the Disaster, and the country still hasn't recovered. Not surprisingly, the renovation of a small park like the one at Lake Romney isn't exactly a top priority. So without anyone attending to it, the place continues to fall apart and decay, like the things that live there in the Zone.

The ride out to Lake Romney was uneventful, but I did get annoyed with Tammy. She kept bugging Jeannie to scan the radio and find the song by that dippy Puddintain band, "You Look Good Enough to Eat." Sadly, Jeannie found it twice and Tammy insisted on singing along with the stupid chorus:

*You look good enough to eat*
*I bet you'd make a tasty treat*
*A little sour, a little sweet,*
*Darlin', you look good enough to eat*

Man, that tune grates on me. The only upside of Tammy's musical obsession was that it made the time go more quickly.

I pulled onto the access road and slowly maneuvered my car around the barricades, dimmed my headlights, and crept over to the lakeshore. There we found a picturesque, sandy area next to where the docks had once been, and I parked. As the guys unloaded the trunk, the girls chatted, laid out blankets, and made drinks.

Before long, much to our chagrin, Tim got out his guitar. There's nothing technically wrong with his playing, but he chooses the dumbest tunes, always including the obligatory, overly dramatic number that ends in a flurry of spastic strumming and tragic vibrato. And then there are those tired old folk songs no one wants to hear, always about sinking ships and lasses from some damn village. Enough already. But it was Tim's birthday, so we were kinder than we otherwise might have been.

As I set up the lanterns, I heard the girls whispering and chuckling a few feet away. I looked toward the Zone and could see the enormous sections of FortiFence that define the Zone's perimeter and that stretch into the distance. We were maybe forty to fifty feet away from the Fence, and as it glistened in the silver light, it almost looked like one of those Christo projects from the pre-Disaster days. I snapped out of my artistic reverie when I actually saw movement through the holes in the Fence. It freaked me out for a sec. No doubt, I thought, a few Horde members were aware of our presence and had gathered to observe us.

Returning to the lantern chores, I mentally dismissed the Horde and concentrated on the whoosh of the waves from the lake. That didn't last long. Our local Horde fan club members began to moan behind the Fence, and I immediately got creeped. The sound is something you don't want to hear, an emphatic mix of agony and anger. Glancing over at my friends, I could tell they heard it, too. Tim stopped playing as we sat there in silence. Finally, everyone ended up looking at me like I had the answer to an unasked question. So I shrugged, made a face, and Tim started playing again.

Ignoring the Horde and their noises, we collectively groaned at Tim's misguided interpretation of a Gordon Lightfoot song, when a strange little pickup whipped into view, with its horn blaring and driving far too fast. As it careened across the sand in our direction, the driver finally hit the brakes, stopping only several feet shy of my car.

I was on my feet in a flash but not before Russ rushed over to chat it up with the truck's driver. After a few words were exchanged between the two of them, Russ laughed and walked toward the tailgate. As I approached the truck, I began to calm down from the sudden intrusion. Abruptly, two guys who I did not recognize stepped out of the vehicle and pulled a tarp off of a very large, kennel-type container in the truck's bed. As the tarp was removed, the kennel appeared to rock back and forth. Russ told us to wait; he'd handle this. So he and the two guys lowered the tailgate, lifted the kennel up and out of the truck, and dropped it roughly onto the sand.

Motioning us to come over, Russ explained to us that these two guys— let's call them Ron and Don for the sake of anonymity—worked at the nearby Shores and ran a surreptitious business on the side. Through them you could "rent" one of those creatures that live at the Shores. You know, the "post-lifers" or whatever they call them. Ron and Don insisted it's a lot better than having a clown or a magician at a party and that the "perishables," as they called them, were usually a lot of fun. Not quite the Horde but close enough to make for a quality, quasi-zombie time. Russ went on to inform us that he'd actually been planning this "surprise" trip to Lake Romney for a couple of weeks because part of it was his birthday present to Tim.

Right about then, I remarked that renting a perishable seemed lame and illegal. Apparently I was the only one who thought so, because my comment generated dirty looks from everyone. Lighten up, they chided.

It's only for a little while, Russ explained, because Ron and Don have got to get the thing back before bed check. Even as the guys opened the kennel, I told Jeannie I didn't like this at all and asked her to stay close, which only made her roll her eyes at me.

I'd never had any friends or family who got infected with the Provo Virus, so I'd never been that close to a victim before. If you watch the Shores ads, you'll notice how there are never any tight shots on the residents. Matter of fact, you rarely see a resident at all.

As the post-lifer wobbled out of the kennel, looking at us with a vacant sort of inquisitiveness, I knew why you rarely saw any of 'em. He'd probably been a guy in his forties when he got bit, or whatever happened. He was dressed in a confusing manner; nothing went together. Plaid pants with a paisley shirt and a striped tie. He looked like he was going to a trailer park prom. But the worst part was—I'm not kidding—his face was only about three-fourths there. In theory, that sounds like most of a face, but I tell ya, it's not. One eye rolled loose in its socket, most of his nose was gone along with his entire right ear, and what was left of his hair was in patches.

Don and Ron instructed the group to treat our "guest" like anyone else. We were told his name was Ben and that he was perfectly harmless; he would probably enjoy a drink or any food we might offer him. He had limited speech skills but would attempt to respond if you talked to him directly. Having relayed that minimal info, Don and Ron said they'd wait in the truck over by the barricades and come back in an hour to pick him up.

As they drove away, Russ, of course, had to live up to his rep. He pushed Tim in the direction of Ben, confiding that Ron and Don had pumped the thing full of so much Blissium back at the Shores that there was no chance of a problem. As if to get the festivities going, Russ threw up his arms and began to dance around Ben, shrieking and cackling like the consummate jackass he is.

The girls giggled as they chastised Russ, which I didn't think sent the right message. I tried to step in and stop Russ, but he managed to run around me and back over to Ben. In all the commotion, Ben tried to slowly spin around in order to keep a watch on Russ; all the while he maintained a semi-smile on his semi-face, his arms reaching out strangely. It almost looked like he wanted to dance with Russ.

Ever the hostess, Becky offered Ben a beer; in response, he sort of nodded and smiled as best he could. As he took the bottle from her, holding it in a precarious manner, Ben tipped the bottle back to what remained of his lips, took a slow gulp, and proceeded to pour most of it on his shirt. Strangely, that seemed to make him happy; he grinned and beamed at us. That got some big laughs from the group, but I just shook my head.

Then Russ nudged Tim and said he was sure that, in Ben, Tim had probably found the perfect audience for his musical stylings. Tim seemed convinced and revealed his own surprise: he'd learned to play "You Look Good Enough to Eat" just for Tammy and plunged right into it. Oh man, not again, I thought:

*You look good enough to eat*
*Although you've got no body heat*
*We'll have some fun between the sheets*
*Darlin', you look good enough to eat*

Tim crooned, Tammy swooned, and Russ continued his spastic beach boogie. I took a look in Ben's direction and his smile had faded; his expression had taken on a look of serious confusion as he stared over at the Zone. It took me a moment to figure out what he was doing; I finally realized he was listening to the Horde. By now, more Horde folk had gathered at the Fence and the volume of their horrible moaning had increased significantly. Perhaps this was an unfortunate side effect from the singing, I thought, or maybe they hate that song, too.

As the Horde began to wail and howl in earnest, it seemed Ben and I were the only two listening to them. Everyone else was so busy singing along with Tim, they were oblivious.

I continued to observe Ben and began to get a bad feeling. He awkwardly sat down on one of the blankets, closed his messed-up eyes, and became very still. A deeply disturbed look replaced the smile on his half-face—a look of remembrance or recognition. Or maybe it wasn't a memory of who he had been but what he had been becoming.

Then Ben opened his eyes, glared at Russ, looked to the sky, and began to wail as he intoned with the nearby Horde. That's when everyone, except Russ, fell silent. It was only when the look on Ben's face turned truly menacing that we realized we were screwed.

And then the shit hit the fan. Ben moved too quickly to be Ben; this couldn't be the same creature. He stood up, hissed in our direction, raced across the sand, and tackled Russ, pinning him facedown on the beach. Russ, thinking it was one of us, cackled and danced on his stomach as Ben sank his teeth into Russ's right shoulder, pulling on the flesh as he did so. When it finally dawned on Russ that the aggressor wasn't one of us, he began to shriek.

Going into autopilot, I grabbed a melon-sized rock and, with a yell that surprised even me, smashed the stone into Ben's skull. He turned, blood dripping from his mouth, snarled at me, and slumped over. I handed the rock to Tim and told him to hit Ben again if he made any move toward Russ. As we kneeled down to check on Russ, we turned him over and could see that Ben had done significant damage in mere moments. Russ laid there with what looked like two or three deep bite wounds just at the top of his shoulder, and as he screamed and panicked, he started to bleed profusely, turning the sand dark around him. The girls yelled loudly enough to get Don's and Ron's attention, and the two showed up in moments, kennel in tow. A thought went through my head: I bet something like this had happened before. As the two rocket scientists wrestled the dazed Ben back into the kennel, I swear to you Ben looked at me and, with a crimson-coated half-smile, whispered, "Munchies."

Things didn't end up so great for Russ. The media would have you believe that all post-lifers are no longer contagious, but that's not true. It turns out a small percentage don't respond to the drugs positively and have the potential to spread the P.V. for as long as thirty days post-Transition. It turned out that Ben had only been at the Shores for about eighteen days.

I will say this: the Shores are nicer than I thought they'd be. Jeannie and I took Becky down there two weeks ago and visited Russ for the first time. I think he remembered us, but it was sure hard to tell. He doesn't look too good. Large chunks of flesh are peeling back from his shoulder and both of his arms, like he's molting. And now he's wearing those same randomly coordinated outfits, too, which is very un-Russ. On the way home, Becky cried the entire time.

Tim called today and told me he'd talked to Admin over at the Shores. Tim continues to feel bad that Russ's birthday present turned into a disaster. As a result, Tim checks in with the facility frequently to get a progress report on his friend who gave the gift that backfired. In any event, the news he got today was a bit much: Admin told him that Russ made a new friend, and it sounds as if they want to be roommates. Yeah, it's Ben, and it seems the two of them enjoy going out dancing together.

I think it would be best if we don't tell Becky.

## THE MIDDAY SNACKLET!

Pressed and formed
MousePouch Snakwiches
with dipping sauce
(m-wave 1.5 minutes)

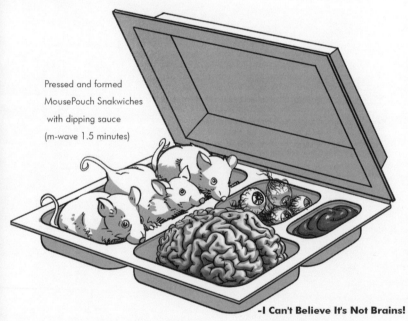

-I Can't Believe It's Not Brains!
-Eyeball candies

# YOU ARE WHO YOU EAT

A few nights ago I was sitting down to watch Del Tenney's classic, *I Eat Your Skin*, and was reminded of how very frightening it must be for those in the Transition. No doubt the majority of you have unflattering zombie images stuck in your heads that have only been reinforced by over-the-top movies such as Mr. Tenney's mess-terpiece. Understandably, it scares the crap out of you that you might end up like those poor souls, clothes in shreds, meandering down a dirt road, feasting on a femur with a vapid look on what remains of your face. As I opened a fresh bag of pork rinds and contemplated your circumstances, I decided that *Z4Z* must redouble its efforts to reassure you that provided you follow the guidance herein, you will not become one of those pathetic creatures.

The title of this chapter is actually deceptive because it's meant to shock you more than anything. Your upcoming culinary world won't include any "who." If you follow this advice, the future will *not* involve you descending on a farmhouse with a pack of your peeps, looking for lunch in all the wrong places. As a result, you'll be able to completely satisfy your hunger, and that farmer's son, little Jimmy, won't become a mid-afternoon snack.

## FOOD, GLORIOUS FOOD

Now that you've got those powerful prescription drugs zipping through your system and you're feeling less sluggish (let's be grateful for *any* sign of progress), it's time to address a course of action on the nutritional front. To begin with, the rules are quite simple: consume anything and everything that's high caloric, high fat, high sugar, high whatever. Indulge. Trust me on this one: you have to cram as much grub as you can into you and do it *now*. Your body is about to burn through calories at an astonishing rate. You're familiar with the phrase "feed a fever"? You're going to need a Bellagio-like bottomless brunch to deal with *this* bad-boy "fever." It's a fact: the quantity of intake will help slow down the effects of the virus. Do you need any more incentive?

It's true that food won't always seem so appetizing over the next several weeks. There may be times when you'll find yourself gasping and groaning; it's understandable. This is a big event and I know it's repeated all too often, but if you don't want to end up all Horde-y, the best action you can take is to keep eating. And limit your diet to normal household rations for now, okay? No free-range yet.

### ℰ BRAINS, BRAINS, THE 𝒵 MAGICAL FRUIT

As you've surely discerned by now, brains are becoming far more fascinating to you, and you recently joined their group on Facebook. Part of this is instinctual: brains are packed with certain nutrients that your evolving body is craving. That delicious mix of soft tissue, enzymes, and proteins would, no doubt, pump you up like a tall, cold can of Rockstar. But we're not serving that drink today. No, what Z4Z is going to do is deliver those same nutrients (and a few more) directly to you. And we do mean "deliver"!

## PUTRISYSTEM™ AND YOU: PERK ME, BABY

The fine folks at Putrisystem want you to know that with a changing body comes changing needs, not the least of which are nutritional. (And boy howdy, nutrition has radically changed in the last few years!) So here's your next perk, compliments of *Z4Z*: a thirty-day introductory supply of Putrisystem products is being shipped to you even as you read this! That's right: you're getting *another* box! If you haven't received it already, you soon will. Here's the beauty part: what you're about to enjoy is a *zero*-obligation trial offer for the new line of Putrisystem meals—P-System Plus™. Breakfast, lunch, snacks, dinner, and dessert—they're all yours for free for thirty days. Now you can spell d-i-e-t without "die"! Lucky you.

No doubt you've seen the commercials featuring TV's former finest extolling the virtues of Putrisystem's basic dieting program. That standard series of products is terrific and very similar to what you'll get, but in this instance you'll be given the revolutionary P-System Plus, designed specifically with the modern post-lifer in mind. Developed with technology from both NASA and D'Oh Chemical, the Plus package is exactly what you need. Whereas the pedestrian line of Putrisystem meals is made to help third-tier celebrities *lose* their tonnage, your products will be all about keeping the weight *on*.

Perhaps the finest aspect of P-System Plus is that it contains the most advanced sports-food technology ever developed—it's rich in advanced nutrients and unusually high in preservatives. "High in preservatives?" you ask. "Isn't that a bad thing?" As it turns out, not always and, most definitely, not a bad thing for *you*.

## PRESERVATION HALL OF FAME

Without getting too technical, the dietary brainiacs behind P-System Plus found that the supposed "bad" additives we've been banning from our food supply for decades can be put to beneficial use for people who find themselves at Disaster-related critical health junctures. People like you. These once-shunned additives can genuinely assist you in sustaining and maintaining your muscle mass and cellular structure, thereby promoting core strength that "trickles up," even into your synaptic pathways. Believe you me, in the upcoming weeks any additional physical or mental assistance will come in mighty handy.

This is precisely why in the P-System Plus recipes you'll find ingredients you haven't seen in years, such as cyclamates, the polysorbate twins, and trans fats, among others. It's like a reunion of friendly faces! And don't forget about several of the tastier shades of artificial colors. Green dye #3 (shiny *and* tasty) and red dye #14 (invigorating)! Finally, who knew potassium bromate could make anything *that much* fluffier or that nitrites and nitrates promote a less-pasty skin tone? It's as if all those allegedly worthless additives have found a fab new home—in you!

But don't just take this writer's word for it. Here's an excerpt from the closing remarks at last year's Laughlin SweetenerCon and Weapons Show. The speaker just happens to be the director of Nutritional Research and Mitigation for Putrisystem, Inc., one Dr. Larry Mengele, who concluded his remarks with: "It is our belief that the P-System Plus will still be a huge moneymaker even *after* litigation costs." Impressive, Larry.

# FOR THE DISCERNING PALATE

Inside your box, you'll find a guidebook and a delicious array of prepackaged foodstuff, with each day's portions already defined and labeled. What a load off, huh? Every product is microwaveable, so you won't be doing much cleanup, either, which is damn good to hear, considering your waning motor skills. But enough of my yammering—here's a sample day's menu for the P-System Plus program:

| | |
|---|---|
| Breakfast | 1 package of P-System HemiDemiSemiEggs (m-wave for 2 minutes)<br>1 can of Sausage 'n Stuff™ (m-wave 1 minute)<br>1 tube of Protein Buddy™<br>1 glass water<br>2 mints |
| Mid-A.M. Snacklet | 3 pressed and formed OSoReal MousePouch Snakwiches™ with dipping sauce (m-wave 1.5 minutes)<br>1 I Can't Believe It's Not Brains™<br>4 eyeball candies |
| Lunch | 2 packages Jowl Subs (m-wave for 1 minute)<br>1 tub SaladSnak™ imitation vegetable substitute<br>1 bag of Cheese Jimmies™<br>1 tube of Protein Buddy<br>2 glasses of water<br>3 mints |

| Mid-P.M. Snacklet | 1 bag of Nice 2 Meat Ya! ™<br>1 tub of Kimchi<br>a dried prune |
|---|---|
| Dinner | 1 package of NearPork™ (m-wave for 2 minutes)<br>1 tub SaladSnak imitation vegetable substitute<br>2 bags of Spudly Dudlies™ (m-wave 1 minute)<br>1 tube of SkullPaste™<br>2 crescent rolls from BagOBread |
| Dessert | 1 scoop of Sweet Intestine Custard<br>4 mints |

Talk about hearty! And that's only one day's example of the month-long goodness you'll get from P-System Plus. Over the course of four weeks, you're guaranteed the balanced nutrition you'll crave going into the Transition and beyond.

## NO SMALL PRINT HERE, BUCKO!

This book takes no formal position regarding what you choose to do after your P-System Plus thirty-day trial is up. However, we strongly suggest that you take advantage of the offer and not go it alone in the kitchen. As this book has stressed, there's a mountain of evidence to indicate that during the first three days you'll experience a hefty decrease in your ability to perform simple tasks. One could extrapolate, then, that the notion of chopping, sautéing, or stir-frying would not be highly recommended; at this point, you could sever a limb with a grapefruit spoon. You absolutely cannot afford to damage yourself now or create opportunities for accidents to happen.

Here's another angle regarding the P-System Plus: should you choose to continue with the program once the trial offer has expired, you won't have to lift a remaining finger. Your meals will be mailed to you every four weeks, your QCard™ *automatically* charged, and shipping and handling will be *free*. Convenience never tasted so good!

If you decide *not* to continue with the program upon the expiration of the trial offer, that's completely your call. (For that matter, if you're still capable of anything that faintly resembles independent thought, then bully for you!) Nonetheless, if you do make such a choice, you *will* need to cancel your subscription to P-System Plus so as not to be charged the full monthly rate. Just call 1-866-NOTHANKS. (A piece of advice: set aside a generous chunk of time for this call, since there are usually ponderous hold times and language issues. The overseas operators still haven't quite nailed down that distinctive post-lifer speech cadence, and this has been known to cause frustration for both parties. And frustration leads to what? Bad behavior, that's right.)

## AVOID THESE LIKE THE PLAGUE!

If you're one of the remarkable few who are still capable of cooking and not just "hunting and gathering," you should be aware that there are supplements and certain types of chow that you should shun. For example:

- Kohlrabi exacerbates dental issues (and Dental Stamps were discontinued last year).

- Creme soda can rupture your trachea.

- Coffee can be rough on what's left of your innards—drink sparingly and go heavy on the QualiMate.

- You will most likely now be lactose intolerant. Violently intolerant.

- While not exactly in the food category, the following advice needs to be reported early on: for dudes, erectile dysfunction drugs should not be used under any circumstances. Recent reports indicate there's a strong likelihood of "breakage," and that sounds like it could hurt. Please learn to value your phallic fella for as long as he's capable of sticking around. And for you dames, here's a benefit worth mentioning: you won't have to worry about your menstrual cycle anymore. Your bodies are so jacked up from the Transition, they've forgotten how to cycle anything!

- Legumes are no longer your friends. 'Nuff said.

- For some reason, Li'l Sally snack cakes (all varieties) cause pica in Methodists.

- Drinking more tap water than what's recommended in the eating plan can lead to seepage, and there are no plans to print Diaper Stamps.

For additional info and if time allows, talk to a medical specialist at a Disaster Kare Kiosk (if you can find one that's open) or a P-System certified sales associate.

## ON A POSITIVE NOTE

To balance out the negatives, here are a few upbeat tips for you.

- Keep taking any vitamins available, especially E and D. And a lot of C. And all of the Bs. Hell, any letters you can get, take 'em.

- Headcheese makes a fine poultice.

- Stop reading nutrition labels; you don't have to care anymore.

- Clam juice mixed with tomato juice makes a snappy drink that takes the edge off certain cravings. Try it!

- Echinacea is best when smoked, but beware: St. John's Wort will *bum you out*!

- Jell-O is good for your bones.

- Cheese and brown rice are superb binding agents, and more than ever, sistuh, you need binding.

- Club soda is a miracle worker with blood and grass stains. (Oh, that's more of a *household* hint, isn't it? More of those later!)

If you think you *will* be preparing your own meals (in spite of being forewarned), check out Appendix A. (Not *that* kind of appendix, silly—the one at the back of the book!) Depending on what's left of your hands, you'll find a handful of mouth-watering recipes (depending on what's left of your mouth), many of which feature brains as the key ingredient. Who loves ya?

## SHOULD I GO "RAW"?

Another resource that might be of genuine help is last year's trendy Dead Sea Diet™, which strongly promotes eating only uncooked foods. Obviously, such a diet takes a hell of a lot of pressure off of your not-so-Iron-Chef kitchen skills. The philosophy behind the Dead Sea Diet is that cooking robs food of its nutrients. By consuming only raw foods, you receive one hundred percent of the vitamins and minerals of whatever (or whomever) you eat. Like Jack LaLanne gone rogue in a produce section, this diet allows you to just mosey on up to that head of lettuce or broccoli (or head of whatev) and bite into it. Eat until you're sated and, bingo, there's your meal. No measuring, no weighing, no kidding! Once again, the convenience is almost too good to be true, although, personally, I'm not sure I could handle a Dead Sea Diet potluck night. Messy.

*Z4Z* offers no guarantee as to the efficacy of the Dead Sea Diet, but we also find no harm in it. (Just make sure you continue to keep your fat content high and remember that there's no such thing as "bad" cholesterol anymore.) An impressive number of consumers have reported that they value the simplicity of this diet and have had considerable success with it. They claim they've benefited from an increased level of energy and a more determined outlook. And, not surprisingly, they find their appetites vastly improved, some even referring to their hunger as "nearly insatiable." Tastes like progress to me!

## DRINK UP!

There's a rumor going around that those in the Transition shouldn't consume alcohol. Nothing could be further from the truth. While regular pain meds won't do a thing for you, ordinary liquor will work wonders. To be completely honest, hooch will *not* help you in the long term; your short term, however, will be hellaciously more tolerable. That striking smell on your skin that develops midway through the second day will be considerably less offensive with a bottle of Sauza socked away. Cocktails are one of the few pleasures that alleviate the sting of the current chaos, so imbibe already.

Experience shows us that Long Island Iced Teas are unusually effective as well as chi-chis, mai tais, and, yes, even zombies. But don't limit yourself to mixed drinks; five or ten shooters will do equally well. (FYI: beer and wine will provide a degree of relief, but this author believes in the efficiency of the hard stuff.) This is not the time to treat your body like it's a temple, because, frankly, by now it's a temple of doom! Besides, very soon you'll be getting Liquor Stamps to support your new habit.

## THE FEW, THE SOBER

No doubt many of you have wrestled with alcohol problems in your former lives, and Z4Z doesn't intend to be insensitive to your prior issues. If you care to maintain your sobriety through the Transition and beyond, here's a beverage you might enjoy: ThugChug 3000™. Yes, the health water/sports drink craze has arrived for post-lifers! TC3K comes with an impressive pedigree. Two-time Olympic tri-athlete-turned-urban-entrepreneur Reggie Neckless (pronounced *nek-uhls*) has burst onto the high-end hydration scene with this powerful and pioneering product. With a potent blend of HGH, B vitamins, taurine, steroids, and crystal-clear water from the Compton Reservoir, this scrappy beverage makes Red Bull look like Sunny frickin' D. Word. Sober post-lifers enjoy it for its clean, crisp taste while totally wasted post-lifers swear it provides a great pick-me-up between benders (not to mention being a top-shelf hangover remedy). Look for ThugChug 3000 in phive phresh phlavas, dawg: Blood Orange™, Barely Berry™, Gangsta Grape™, Lemon Pop-a-Cap-in-Your-Ass™, and Liver. As Reggie says, "Try one cold and you'll be sold."

And in case anyone's interested, TC3K goes great with vodka. Or gin.

## MAYBE AN EVENING OUT?

Finally, because both companies have been good friends to *Z4Z*, I feel compelled to mention the two big restaurant chains that cater to diners of your ilk: Gristle's Steakhaus™ and Cap'n Ash's Seafood Fortress.

Bob Gristle is a former CFO of QualiCorps and one of my best buds. A few years back, upon deciding he wanted to explore his entrepreneurial side, Bob stepped down from his high-paying corporate job. Having recognized the need for a quality dining experience *inside* the Shores facilities, Bob opened his first Gristle's a mere three years ago in a Shores outside of what used to be Dallas. As the chain continues to expand into every remaining state and Safe Area, Bob's vision has led to the greatest restaurant success story post-Disaster. And with the recent move to expand outside of the Shores, even regular folks (like who you used to be) are now enjoying down-home grub at Gristle's.

 So why is Gristle's so popular? Bob explains it like this:

> *We're currently the only post-lifer establishment where you can get, under one roof, authorized entrées from either P-System Plus or the Dead Sea Diet. Matter of fact, each program has its own page on our menus. Additionally, we offer old-fashioned goodness and value with a variety of semi-steaks and sorta-salads. At Gristle's, you'll find more to drool over than at any other restaurant that will allow you inside. And I don't care what that idiot Ash tries to tell you, ours is the premiere dining experience for Mr. and Mrs. Recently Bitten. Remember our motto, "Let's pretend it's beef!"*

It's also worth noting that Bob's list of humanitarian efforts is as impressive as his cuisine. He has served as chairman of the Provo Virus Kids Kommittee; he was an Accomplished Fellow at the Q-Academy of Food Sciences; and just recently he was appointed as the Secretary of Steak to the President's Council on Future Meats. I'm proud to know him. Hey, Bob, save a place for me—I'll be by tonight!

Where Gristle's caters to a slightly upscale demographic, Cap'n Ash's Seafood Fortress appeals to the budget-minded. It's a nautical-themed joint that promotes the versatility and scrumptiousness of various species of what were affectionately called "trash fish." Once thought to be of no epicurean use whatsoever, many of these fish are now prominently featured at Cap'n Ash's. Let me tell you, what Ash does with a lamprey eel is nothing short of artistic, and you can have a ball picking out your own from the sizeable tank in the lobby. And don't forget to try the Sculpin Sticks; my friends just love 'em. Finally, not only is Cap'n Ash's easy on the pocketbook, but everyone will love the monstrous animatronic squid that adorns the foyer. You won't be disappointed, and the taste will disappear from your mouth within twenty-four hours, tops.

## IT'S A LOT TO DIGEST

You've had a ton of info thrown at you quickly and you may be, quite frankly, somewhat overwhelmed. No need to be. Remember, initially you won't have to do jack in order to get the help you need. The P-System Plus shipment should arrive any minute now.

In summing up, you only have two ideas to remember from this chapter: 1) spend your stamps freely; and 2) keep your caloric intake way up.

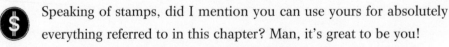

Speaking of stamps, did I mention you can use yours for absolutely everything referred to in this chapter? Man, it's great to be you!

Now that you've been set on the right culinary track, let's consider the most appropriate exercise program for you. See you on the mats!

# REBOOT CAMP:

## EXERCISE AND YOU

Now that you're stylin' on the victuals front, it's time to address your very real, very urgent exercise needs.

You're probably thinking, "But you *just* said I need to eat a lot and retain calories. Won't exercise negate that?" Alas, food is only *part* of the equation that's going to keep you intact; you still need to get up and move around, even if such motion resembles nothing more than organized stumbling.

Indeed, it's imperative that you incorporate regular exercise into your everyday life, but it's most important in the upcoming hours and days. Some "humans" in your condition do yoga or follow one of those wacky cardio-boxing regimens (both are discussed later in this chapter), while others choose to aerobically roll around on the ground and weep. Frankly, your preference matters far less than your level of commitment. During this next critical phase, a lazy attitude can lead to increased stiffening, and this is never good.

## OUT GOES THE BAD AIR, IN GOES THE BAD

Before we get to specific exercises, it's important to first talk about breathing. I believe it was Ethel Merman who said, "I breathe when I have to." Sure, that was great for her, but some of us (i.e., *you*) don't have that luxury. You need to be aware of how (and if) you're breathing as you begin your chosen mode of exercise. Breathing plays a vital role in promoting proper fitness and, personally, it's my favorite involuntary function. Learning to breathe correctly during your workout will help build your stamina (I use the term loosely, of course).

Don't be surprised if the ol' breathing routine isn't quite as "auto" as it once was. You may need to intermittently remind your functions how to do their thing by the use of gentle verbal "triggers" such as "inhale, exhale, inhale, exhale." Like placing jumper cables on crusty battery posts, the repetition of such prompts will eventually force the ignition that is your nervous system to get a clue and turn over. Try the aforementioned triggers when necessary and attempt to breathe at a consistent level. And for cryin' out loud, keep your battery posts cleaner.

## AS IT TURNS OUT, FITNESS IS A STRETCH!

Any exercise routine should always begin with basic stretching. This loosens the ligaments, prevents you from blowing an O-ring, and helps fend off that wretched rigor mortis. If your personal stretching routine is done correctly, you may not need any other exercise plan. As a matter of fact, the President's Council on Diet, Fitness, and Jerky recommends that those in Transition begin by limiting their workouts to three ten-minute stretching sessions a day.

Stretch whenever you'd like, but for best results the sessions should be spaced equally apart. For example, create a schedule such as: 8:00 a.m., 12:00 p.m., 4:00 p.m. A plan like this should provide a solid workout and still leave you available for Springer at 5:00 p.m. Of course, stretching *before* eating is always advised. Too much sloshing around after a big meal is not hot.

I don't know about you, but I'm all about exercises I can do while lying down. And that's *all* that's being asked of you—lie down on your back and gradually move your limbs around. It may be that you're feeling a smidgen rigid, and you definitely want to get those knots out before they set in. A fabulous jumping-off point for stretching is the "Floor Angel," an exercise that's all the rage with Transitioneers because it mimics the fanciful behavior of our wintry youth when we made snow angels. While you're splat on the floor, move your arms and legs up and down in the same manner you did on those snow days of yesteryear.[17] Exhilarating and a kick!

There's no need to go hog wild and get all Cirque du Whatever-ay contortionist about your stretching. No inverted dangling from block-long silk draperies; such extremes are not needed here. Simple, gentle movements are really all that's required. Begin with just the daily ten-minute sessions, and gauge how those feel before considering additional exercises. It's better to start slow—like a Lenny kind of slow.

---

17. ● That is, except for you poor schmucks who grew up in the desert. What did you make—dust angels? Sandmen?

## ⚡ SAY "YO" TO YOHIMBE ⚡

Before we crank it, and in order to maximize your upcoming cutting-edge workout, here are a few products worth hitting up. By the way, all three interact perfectly with your Putrisystem meals and are stamp-friendly:

- *MegaMass Dyno-ZPlex™*. Athletes will tell you, they're only as good as their nutritional powders.[18] That's precisely why you might want to consider using MegaMass Dyno-ZPlex before your next intense training session or lone push-up. Its blend of creatine, amino acids, yohimbe bark, and dried, crushed organs will take you to the next level of fitness. This is one product you've oblon-gotta get!

- *VunderBar™*. At long last, a nutrition bar made for the hectic post-lifer post-lifestyle. Rich in fiber, wood pulp, and Blissium, VunderBar makes it easy to stay calm, while satisfying those between-meal cravings. Consume one today!

- *M-Balm™*. A formula so potent, it can work on you! Apply M-Balm to achy joints or torn tendons after your workout, and you'll notice a real difference. Feel the pain almost melt away.

## GETTING UP IS HARD TO DO

 When you *are* ready to move on from stretching, I recommend you start by simply sitting up. Not sit-ups—just sitting up. That's right,

---

18. And those injections they get from that bald guy with the eye patch in the IMRV.

too much lying around can make you sulky and sleepy. Sitting upright is the first step to the rest of your workout. Doesn't that feel better? No—don't slide back down! Get up! The drugs should be kicking in any second, and combined with the P-System fare, you should be sensing a decrease in your bloodlust by now. You have no excuses. So sit up!

## FOR A LEANER, LESS-DEAD LOOK

Okay, then. That's better.

If after a day or two of sitting up and stretching, you find you're craving more physical exertion and would like to "pump it up," consider these three options.

### ZeeBo™

Now *you* can do your own version of that sensational red-hot boxing workout, reimagined for guys and gals like you. In this deluxe 19-DVD boxed set, ZeeBo's creator, Jerry Jack, takes you through hour after hour after hour of his new, low-to-no-impact program. On disc 1, you'll learn extensively about Jerry's can-do philosophy as he relays most of his childhood in real time (his fourth year is particularly disturbing). On disc 6, Jerry's finally got you into the gym after driving around his Brentwood 'hood and showing off his vintage car collection. By the time you get to the life-changing disc 12, he's got you doing things you didn't think possible. You'll raise your knees—sort of! You'll almost deflect an imaginary punch! You'll amble in place with the best of 'em! And here's a Jerry Jack promise: you'll see *genuine* results with ZeeBo within 180 days, or your stamps will be refunded in full! (Minus shipping and handling, of course.)

## YOGA

If the ZeeBo system seems a bit ambitious at this time, consider yoga. Yes, yoga.

Now don't get all judgmental and think you'll be expected to hit the bong, too. Yoga's not just for hippies anymore. Everyday citizens are learning that a basic asana goes a long way, and in your case these "adapted asanas" are the shiznit!

For example, the traditional Lotus position has been modified to become the effective "Lotus Lite." Several painful aspects of the original Lotus have been eliminated so that in the Lotus Lite you can simply sit with your arms and legs in a comfortable position. Now attempt to concentrate (or "meditate," as we'll soon learn) and focus on your breathing. How shallow is it? Are both lungs working and intact? Did you just exhale?

In addition, the "Downward Dining Dog" offers a challenge for the individual who wants to press a little harder. When ready, assume the standard push-up position and hold it in place. Lower your neck as if you're trying to drink from a bowl and then freeze. How's your breath control? Again, try to clear your mind, which should be a cakewalk. If this asana is held fully for the suggested twelve minutes, it will tax every bone left in your body. (A word of caution: build up to this exercise slowly. No need to pop a femur by being overanxious.)

Lastly, "The Stranded Trout" emphasizes the supine position; from here, the subject performs a series of gentle flops. (A yoga mat is highly recommended—a bed works nicely, too.) This asana facilitates relaxation, inner harmony, and accommodates an increasing lack of cartilage.

## OOZIN' TO THE OLDIES™

If you can track down and order an old VHS copy online, you might enjoy the *Oozin' to the Oldies* workout, developed by '70s child star and exercise guru Beany Ramirez. Apparently this videotape has quite the cult following among post-lifers. Fans report not only enjoying swaying in their studio apartments to the corny classics of the past, but also seem to be mesmerized by Beany's sparkly shorts and distinctive 'fro-mullet. Go for it. I'm all about whatever gets your last few pints of blood pumping!

# SPORTS, PERHAPS?

Maybe you're one of countless individuals who, in your old life, enjoyed playing sports by yourself or with others. You lived for those weekend flag football games with the guys, that pick-up round of hoops down at the park, or a summer game of soccer with the girls. Well, I hate to break it to you, but such activities will no longer work for you. Anything that involves potential full contact is now taboo; you've got *fragile* written all over you. Remember that law of physics: velocity plus mass equals a honkin' booboo and a visit to the emergency room! So, pally, nix the "big six": football, hockey, soccer, basketball, rugby, and baseball. But don't get hinky on me; there are *several* options that have proven to be hits with both genders of post-lifers.

## GOLF

If you were already a golfer, great. If not, now's your chance to hit the links and learn this allegedly lively international sport. It's one terrific way to get out in the world and "walk" away your worries, and the somewhat sluggish pace is pitch-perfect for post-lifers. For those who don't care to walk the course, use one of the modified carts, as long as your hand-to-eye coordination is still adequate.

You'll be pleased to learn that every Scarlet Shores has a challenging three-hole course (complete with the ParMuch™ feature), which you can play over and over 'til you're dizzy with delight. To me, there's nothing quite like shooting a few holes to clear the mind. The smell of wet grass and caustic fertilizers is a revitalizing combo.

## SHUFFLEBOARD

There is a strange misconception regarding this sport—that it's strictly for blue hairs, cruise-ship-goers, and Thurston Howell types. Nothing could be further from the truth. Shuffleboard can be a competitive, gritty game that involves strategy and finely tuned motor skills. You'll get a solid aerobic workout from bending over repeatedly and lurching up and down the court. But careful with those cues—no jousting allowed!

## T-BALL

Have you ever seen how much fun little kids have while playing T-ball, squealing as they hit the ball four feet, then scampering around the bases? You, too, can enjoy that level of merriment, but you've got to give T-ball a chance; no looking down the remainder of your nose at it. With the smallest of attitudinal adjustments, soon you, too, could be swinging wildly and running the bases like a toddler. Batter up!

## BADMINTON

The shuttlecock flies your way, you raise your racquet, ace the shot, and win the game! Sound like fiction? Absolutely not. Badminton is one of the most popular sports among active post-lifers, especially those who can still lift their arms. Maybe it's the fierce dynamic of the sport or the doubles play, or maybe it's the mesmerizing movement of the shuttlecock. Whatever the attraction, there's no denying what a great workout you can get while meeting a few soon-to-be friends. And don't worry: the pace at the Shores is not that frenetic. No Olympic overachievers here. The Shores' brand of badminton is a friendlier version tailored more for a social setting. One thing to remember: if you do play doubles, no staggering into one another—that's considered poor sportsmanship. Save that full-body contact for your next late-night hook-up!

## GLOW-BUMPER BOWLING

Black lights, inflatable bumpers in the gutters, cool shoes, cold beer. Does it get any better than that? Now, with the availability of four-pound balls, I envision three-hundred games for even the most run-of-the-mill bowler. Scarlet Lanes proudly offers up this happenin' hybrid of bowling five nights a week. They've even got leagues and computerized scoring. Good thing, too—math harder now. Between the brewskis (Schlitz on tap!) and your obscenely high scores, you'll walk away feeling something like a winner.

## HUNTING

No, you don't get to shoot an actual gun, but you *will* be given a nifty laser pointer in the shape of a ray gun to pretend you're zapping your prey! It's the thrill of the hunt without the muss and fuss. Once you're armed and decked out in your awesome camouflage gear, you'll be allowed full access to an exclusive area of the Shores' petting zoo. I don't need to remind you to be kind to the animals, and should one happen to bite you, there will be *no* biting back. Violators will be issued a stern stamp penalty.

## THE ROCK WALL

You've seen 'em on TV and probably in one of those sprawling outdoor-life megastores with a bass the size of a Buick nailed above the entrance. Check it out—now *you're* going to have access to a climbing wall 24/7. Righteous. Every Shores has its own custom wall that's certain to test your skills. Standing at a towering fourteen feet and made of solid Nerf, you'll be hard-pressed to scale this muthuh the first time. Even so, you'll be wearing the mandatory Happy Harness™, because your safety is, of course, a major concern at the Shores. Rappel away.

## FISHING

Not so much of a sport as a sporty activity, fishing still can be quite the workout, especially at the mini-ponds at the Shores. Please note: all anglers are discouraged from jumping into the ponds and grabbing whatever aquatic life is available. You are asked to use a rod and reel while discovering the excitement of pulling in a real honker. Go ahead, load up your stringer with perch, sunfish, and bluegill—all the big guns are waiting. And if you're squeamish about baiting the hook yourself, staffers are ready to slap on a worm for you for a nominal stamp charge. And you spear fishermen, get one of the modified BBQ forks from the rental shed and have at it!

## AND OTHER FORMS OF RECREATION, TOO

I've been told by several activity directors from different Shores locations that they're seeing all sorts of innovative leisure interests catching on. An extremely "slow-impact" version of Ping-Pong is a current craze along with a form of junior cricket. And you thought those cricket matches were interminable before! Plus, there's a modified take on horseshoes that's developed a following. The stakes are placed a mere six feet apart, making it much easier for post-lifers to have a snowball's chance of scoring. And, finally, a type of lawn curling has been developed that seems to be going over like gangbusters. The brooms have been replaced with rakes and the stones with, well, rocks. Apparently the competitors just *love* swinging those rakes around and around, trying to move those damn rocks! Whatever floats your boat, I say.

Given the above litany of groovy activities, your athletic options are numerous in the post-life. Game on!

## ARE THERE ANY ACTIVITIES TO BE AVOIDED?

Glad you asked. Besides the big six, there are activities to be eschewed by men and women alike. Briefly, they are:

- Aquacizing—Chlorine can be hard on what's left of your skin. Stick to swimming in ponds or any other body of fresh water you can get your appendages in.

- Fencing—I don't care if the sword points are blunted, you don't need to be stabbing or getting stabbed in any manner.

- Skiing—Are you kidding me? Your joints would fly apart within minutes, whether in water or snow. Want a thrill? Watch an extreme ski movie. *Whee.*

- Cycling—Unless you're talking tricycling, don't bother. Balance is an important part of cycling and yours will be lacking.

- Racquet sports other than badminton—Tennis moves too fast, and you could really get banged up in racquetball and squash—well, you never even played squash. You thought it was elitist crap, remember?

- Pole vaulting—Again, did you ever do this in your old life? Think about it: you're far more likely to impale yourself than go sailing over the bar. And while we're on the subject of Olympic-style events, you'll need to bail on the high jump (highly unlikely), shot put (not), javelin (injurious), and discus (let's not discuss it). Oh, and forget gymnastics altogether.

- Bull riding—Those vibrations could shatter your bones, and there aren't any bulls in the petting zoos. Besides, the sport is sooooo very white.

- Running—You can try it, but, realistically, you're looking at an activity that's more akin to speed-crawling. Avoid so as not to get demoralized.

- Triathlon—Yeah, right.

- Hang gliding—Get a grip.

- *Real* boxing—Are you nuts?

- Martial arts—No. Like, really no.

## GOTTA HAVE THE GEAR!

Regardless of what method of workout you choose, you're encouraged to dress properly. I know you may no longer be overly concerned with how you look during a workout, but your self-image should stay as puffed up as possible. No need to drop a ton of kwan on velvet jogging suits or mink-lined gym bags; leave that to Diddy. And don't go wasting your hard-earned stamps on one of those space-age wrist heart monitors—they're not going to be able to detect a discernible tick in you.

Research has shown that looking good *will* actually aid you in getting a better workout. Any items from the Second Skin™ athletic line are particularly apropos for post-lifers. The way the products help hold you together is, of course, invaluable, but the finest feature of Second Skin is that all separates come in distinctive colors and patterns that can be effortlessly coordinated. And the bloodstain-resistant, tight Zylon™ mesh is truly a miracle fiber. No more overnight soaking of clothes; these duds can take the splatters and come out spotless the next morning.

## YOU'RE BEING GROOMED FOR THE FUTURE!

Mark my words: exercising is a pain in the petoot, but you *will* feel better when you make yourself "just do it." Summon up the conviction of a full-page Nike ad, and get ready to look and feel better.

Speaking of looking better, it's time for skin care and grooming tips. And a little something to help that ever-evolving odor of yours, too!

1. The Dumas

2. The Kent

3. The Douche

OFFICIAL HAIRSTYLES
FOR
POST-LIFERS

4. The Screech

5. The Goober

6. The Zombie

We specialize
in cutting hair
correctly . . .
Because you
can't grow it
anymore.

# YOU CAN HEAL YOUR POST-LIFE:

## CARE AND GROOMING

I guarantee that I'll always give it to you straight, so here goes: the one aspect of your being that will take the biggest hit during the Transition is your appearance. I'm sure you've already noticed a degree of degradation; it happens quickly in the first day or two. Your skin is taking on a distinct gray-green tone. Your eyes look like you're coming off of a two-week peyote binge in Baja. And the hair loss—ah, the hair loss. This seems to be a variable that impacts certain folks more than others. The good news is, looking great is still somewhat within your reach and without resorting to the dreaded comb-over. The upcoming pointers will enhance your exterior and, along with a series of product recommendations, benefit your cause big-time.

## YOU'RE SO VEINY, YOU PROBABLY THINK THIS BOOK IS ABOUT YOU

The primary issue this chapter addresses is dealing with any lingering sense of vanity you might be clinging to. Time to say buh-bye to that. The day *will* come when you'll feel better about your looks again (or at least not as miserable about them), but that may take awhile. If you're one of those narcissistic types who lingers in front of mirrors, primping and fussing, or take any opportunity to admire your reflection, you'll need to ditch that habit now (and I'm *so* not kidding). In the immediate future, mirrors will *not* be your friends, and your reflection will be a traitorous bastard. Again, until such time as we can minimize the damage and make you closer to presentable, it's a dandy idea not to monitor your progress.

## SUNSHINE ON MY SHOULDERS MAKES ME CRANKY

As for advice, here's a biggie to begin with: stay out of the sun. Even in your prior life, prolonged exposure to the sun was not the best call and could lead to George Hamilton. From now on, going after that golden glow is downright deranged. There is not an SPF in the known universe that has a high enough rating for someone in the Transition.[19] To be clear, I'm not talking about a vampire-type reaction where sunshine turns you into dust. Don't be silly—vampires don't exist.[20] If you choose to subject yourself to direct doses of those luxurious solar death-rays, you'll notice an almost instantaneous blistering of your skin. Such wounds are slow to heal, not to mention they increase your capacity to be cantankerous. If you absolutely must go out, cover yourself from head to toe, preferably in a Klaatu-ish silvery, reflective fabric. Still, I beseech you: don't do additional damage to yourself during this time; stay inside with the TV and a good book (like *Z4Z*).

---

19.  QualiTone once marketed an SPF 1700, but the molasses-like material never caught on.
20.  Unless you happen to be one, in which case look for next year's *V4V*!

## BEAUTY TIPS POUR VOUS

As promised, this chapter provides grooming techniques and nightly bedtime beauty rituals to help you cope with the loss of not only skin tone but skin itself. We forget how valuable ye olde epidermis is until it starts to fall off. And once it's gone, baby, it is *gone*. No Wolverine healing powers here, friends. But have no fear—what follows will help you retain a majority of whatever you've got left.

The first thing you need is R-E-S-T. I know I told you to jet through this book in record time, but you still need quality downtime. Any Borg will tell you that the regenerative nature of sleep is one of the best all-around solutions for nurturing your body. Don't let stress or your incessant moaning get in the way, either. If you need extra meds, chug a few HammerMe's from a bottle in your CareBox. And screw the dosage warnings; like somehow you're going to feel *worse*?

Speaking of the CareBox, now would be a good time to check out one of those Hungry Boy MeatMasks that's tucked away inside. As nighttime beauty treatments go, these hombres excel when it comes to effectiveness and ease of use. Prior to bedtime, whip that MeatMask out of the fridge, rip it out of the packaging, and as you retire for the evening, drape it over your face. Make sure you press down on the mask's greasy edges; you want to cover as much skin as possible. While you rest, the patented blend of mammal paste and natural oils works on pore redefinition and rejuvenates your "troubled" complexion, giving you an appealing pasty glow the very next day.

Indeed, as far as beauty products go, you're covered. Your favorite store (and mine) carries the entire Gentleman Q™ and Lady Q™ lines of personal products and grooming utensils. These items come highly recommended and, naturally, are easy on the stamps. A number of lotions, shampoos, and conditioners for each gender are available to address the particulars of post-lifers' skin types. (Let's face it—some of us are simply oilier than others.)

A cautionary note: it seems that quite a few companies are trying to penetrate the post-lifer consumer market with inferior products. Avoid the following at all costs:

- Gee, Your Hair Doesn't Stink So Much
- The Four-Hour Miracle Treatment
- Anything by Dedken

All are strongly discouraged. Don't fall for their fakery.

The post-life presents unique challenges when it comes to sprucing yourself up, so make sure you've got the right tools for the job. One of the most popular is the Sculptulette™, which resembles a shrunken spatula. When used in conjunction with the Q-Line brand of HeadPutty™, your head will recoup a convincing, nearly human shape and size. Simply push a generous amount of HeadPutty into any facial cracks or divots that are currently bothersome, manipulate the putty to your satisfaction with the Sculptulette, allow approximately forty-five minutes for it to dry—and voila!—you'll sort of look like how you used to. Any excess putty can be removed with a petite piece of sandpaper or steel wool. Remember, HeadPutty—from the same folks that bring you BoobPutty™ and ButtPutty™.

Now let's chat it up with the ladies. The makeup line that comes most recommended is VigorMortis™, the revolutionary cosmetics by Graybelline developed specifically for the modern female post-lifer. VigorMortis attempts to restore the color to your cheeks and elsewhere. It offers a complete series of products, including foundations, blushes, eye shadows, mascaras, and cheek gunk. Used as directed, the VigorMortis collection will give girls a radiance that will approximate a healthy look ("healthy" being a relative term). It's important to note that each VigorMortis product is cruelty-free, meaning that none have been tested on dead animals. And all are endorsed by PETZ™ (People for the Ethical Treatment of Zombies).

## HEY, HOW ABOUT COSMETIC SURGERY?

How do I put this kindly? No.

You see, post-Disaster, there aren't nearly as many medical professionals available. We lost a significant number of doctors to bitings and to mass exoduses to the golf courses of both the Bahamas and Scotland.

Several top-notch companies now offer, exclusively for the post-lifer market, a number of spirited colognes and playful parfums. Each is designed to help you with your personal stench issues, which are a result of that nasty bit of decomposition you're experiencing. Babes seem to be digging on Consommé, from Kalvin Klone, a gelatin-based fragrance you can find conveniently in any soup aisle. The once stalwart company Avon is back with Jugular for Men, the new standard for post-lifuh playuhs. Additionally, dudes are "feeling" Brut and Hai Karate once again, supposedly because of their (continued on page 102)

dependable, distinctively heavy scents. Chanel No. 178(a) is another, not-so-subtle entry for the ladies that's sure to captivate the fellas while taking the edge off of that odor. The days of dabbing are over—use any of these products liberally and frequently.

Additionally, the government appropriated thousands of professionals to deal with the massive medical issues that remain from the Disaster. Simultaneously, the Feds passed a temporary law forbidding cosmetic surgery, deeming it to be "frivolous."[21] Lastly, the Shores hired a bunch of the white-coated buggers, too.

**❗** So what I'm getting at is, no one's available to do that modest amount of cosmetic work on which you've set your sights. No liposuction (like you need *that*!), tit job, chin job, bone job, face lift, ass lift, mentoplasty, rhinoplasty, chemical peel (again, so not needed), or tummy tuck. Sorry. Of course, you *could* go south of the border, but word has it they've got Horde problems of their own. From what *I* hear, post-lifers are, on occasion, being used in the arenas down there to offset a bull shortage. Not to mention, the health-care system in Mexico is not stamp-compatible with ours.

However, in place of such surgeries, *Z4Z* provides you with realistic options to consider, and all are available through several, shall we say, "unofficial channels."

---

21. Can you believe that? That's the word they used—*frivolous*. Seems insensitive, doesn't it?

## FAUXTOX™

The *last* thing you need in your body right now is another damn toxin! Because of this, pharma giant ChemKwik has developed a synthetic bovine bio-product, Fauxtox. Don't ask me about the components of Fauxtox; somehow those ChemKwik geniuses found a way to re-create the firming and rejuvenating properties of Botox *without* the toxicity. Delivered by injection just like Botox, Fauxtox will deaden ("flatten" would be more accurate) an area a lot more effectively than that wussy Botox ever dreamed of doing. And the effects last a lot longer, too (allow up to nine months), depending on the dosage. If you think your wrinkles or wounds need a little extra smoothing, ask around and I'm sure you can find someone to administer Fauxtox under the table for a few stamps.[22] A piece of advice: pop five or six HammerMe's right before you get an injection, 'cause that suckuh is gonna sting!

## BRITEBROWN™

If they're not already funky, your teeth are heading in that direction. In the weeks to come, they'll lose their glistening whiteness and turn a dark, chocolaty color. Cheer up, because BriteBrown Teeth Lightening and Lazik Clinics™ have come up with a solution. If you want your choppers to return to a more alluring beige, seek out these dental wizards at any of their four hundred nationwide locations. And as their name suggests, as long as you're there, why not have them redo your vision and reseat your eyeballs? BriteBrown's motto: "We'll work with whatever you've got left!"

# LOOK—WE'VE GOT COMPANY!

All of the above counsel is perfectly sound, but professional beauticians are always able to offer you the best advice on all issues. Therefore, I've sought out two specialists in this field to contribute to this chapter. Let's meet 'em!

---

22. But *I* didn't tell you that, okay?

First up, I'm pleased to welcome Mr. Romar Porvel, the winner of last year's harebrained hair-themed reality show, *Cut-Up*™. As a result of his triumph on that show (shown exclusively on Scarlet TV), Romar is now touring the nation on behalf of his book, *What The Hell Is That On Your Head?* and his new CD of reinterpreted Celtic classics, *Irish Stylist*. Not only is Mr. Porvel signing CDs and books on a tour of bookshops, but in his spare time he donates his evenings to local shelters, coifing and berating the hairdos of homeless women. Romar is a fount of very strong ideas and is not afraid of expressing himself, so Reader, you would be well served to take in an earful of his opinions.

*Thank you. It gives me an inordinate amount of pleasure to be here. You see, like many others, the post-lifer cause has become near and dear to me, especially after my brush with death during the Great Valley Descent four years ago. Those things came over the hill and were onto Ventura before I could say TRESemmé. Girl, they were chowing down on my clients while I was still packing my blow dryer! Uh-huh. I didn't even have the foil off that gal's head before those things were unwrapping her like satay.*

*But let's get to the point: there are a lot of products available for post-life skin care, but a veritable dearth of quality hair-care items. It's as if the major manufacturers collectively rolled over and surrendered on this front. Maybe the ratty appearance of post-lifers' hair gave them such pause they refused to muster the effort. Hell, I don't know. Well, I'm here to tell you that, as of today, I'm releasing my new series of hair products expressly created for you: R. Porvel's Twi-Life*™. *With Twi-Life shampoos and conditioners, guys and gals will experience:*

- *Hair that's less ratty and with fewer bugs*
- *Improved texture and manageability*
- *Extra additives for more scalp control*
- *A look that resembles shine*

*Our patented industrial/botanical formula gives relief from that greasy, smelly rat's nest on your head, replacing your "don't" with an absolute "do." Check it out. Your hair will be better looking, and it won't fall out as quickly, either! Put a smile on your hair with Twi-Life!*

*When first using my shampoo, heed the requirements of the initial application. It's imperative you rinse and repeat. Then rinse and repeat. And again. And again. For best results, that first use should consist of eight to ten consecutive shampoos. That way, you'll be sure to eliminate every last bit of dried fluid, gnat, or bone from your skullular region. Immediately follow that ritual with my Twi-Life conditioner, which calls for one solid hour of conditioning. My revolutionary blend of lemon grass, lavender, and industrial solvents really needs a chance to get in there and do its thing. After one hour, rinse thoroughly; I mean, like an OCD kind of thoroughly! Dry with a soft towel and style to your liking. Should you need help on the styling front, try hitting up R. Porvel's Sculpting Jamm™. That is one rockin' concoction of polymers that will lock down your look.*

Well done, Romar. I know you're due back at the shelter, so thanks again for your time and contribution.

Now let's bring in our resident skin-care specialist, Oblivion, for a quick lesson about how best to reenergize your epidermis. Oblivion comes to us from Toronto, where she runs her Académie of Skin Care and Bait Emporium. Like Romar, she's also a humanitarian, offering cosmetic advice to members of the last-known indigenous tribe in Brazil. Listen up.

*Well, I hate to be the contrarian here, but I don't find the Q Products to be of any real value. Too many ingredients and they're manufactured in Dayton. When you think beauty, do you think Dayton? No duh. So if you want your skin to return to its former natural state, throw that crap away. All you need is the following homemade moisturizing formula that, by the way, doubles as a kicky dipping sauce:*

*1 cup Miracle Whip (the real stuff, no knockoffs)*
*1 tbsp. ketchup*
*1 tsp. Worstershire sauce*
*1 egg*
*1 tsp. olive oil*

*Mix it all together and ladle it onto your face. It's sooooo easy. Relax and read a copy of Dedbook while you let this concoction soak into your skin for about a half an hour. Wash it off with warm water. Do this for two or three days and you'll see a real difference. Even your friends will notice an unusual sheen to your skin, and the smell is just this side of scrumptious. If you like how this moisturizer makes you look, pass it along to your friends. They'll thank you later.*

*And, ladies, as far as makeup goes, I'll say to you what I say to my indigenous customers: always aim for the au naturel look, which usually requires quite the array of products! Always begin with a simple foundation and layer it up to taste. Again, you don't need all that specialized and pricey Q-crap; the cheaper and more traditional products will work just fine. And always remember that, with makeup, there is such a thing as too much. A tarted-up look might get you a night or two with an ice road trucker but little else.*

As always, Oblivion, I'm all about anything that includes Miracle Whip. Thanks for the tips!

## YOU'RE LOOKING WAY BETTER NOW—YES, WAY

I can hardly recognize you! You look great! I can't believe you're the same individual who first lurched into this chapter. The change is downright Kafkaesque!

Let me once more remind you how extremely important it is to avoid lollygagging between chapters. No, really. The clock is ticking and the Transition waits for no one.

But first, please take a brief moment to listen to this encouraging message from one of our fine sponsors...

# WELCOME TO SCARLET SHORES!

You've been deemed suitable for a future like no other! And at Scarlet Shores Assisted Post-Living Centers™ that future begins today!

When you first enter any of our dozens of gleaming facilities, you'll encounter beauty on a scale that's rarely seen and lush appointments wherever you look. Soothing voices, bright colors, and pretty arrows direct you to your destinations. Everywhere you go, you'll meet folks just like you who have been given the opportunity to be productive, active citizens once more.

Scarlet Shores is where all of this happens for YOU.

Each Scarlet Shores is a certified "green community"—and that has nothing to do with the tint of your skin! Here, every component of life is almost in ecological balance. What this means is that all traces of any dangerous residue that remained beneath and within these former federal correctional facilities and Superfund sites have been completely removed. And that means a 100 percent nontoxic, healthy home, which is more than can be said for most communities these days.

Just consider the Scarlet Shores staff: our employees (or "providers," as we call them) go through an exhaustive, two-week training course in order to be a part of your Shores family. You'll find them to be not only courteous, but forceful and effective when needed. Each staff member is equipped with the latest in anti-Horde combat skills and technologies, because your safety (and ours) is important.

Imagine what lies ahead for you:

• Your very own opulent 12' x 18' studio apartment complete with mini-kitchen, VibroBunk™, and a roll of quarters on the house.

- Leisurely dinners at any Gristle's Steakhaus or Cap'n Ash's Seafood Fortress. Be sure to try the "Bloomin' Livers™"!

- Sumptuous afternoons at the Skin Spa™ or QCasino™.

- Complimentary ground transportation provided by our glistening fleet of ShuffleCrafts, the vehicles that move slightly faster than you!

- Field trips to the Shores' own Quali-Ko™, where you'll be free to spend your Liquor, Drug, Garment, and other Stamps.

- The Shores' own online (and off-line) dating service, Stiff Competition™.

- Twenty full hours a day of customized post-lifer broadcasting and available for free only on—Scarlet TV!

- Festive afternoons in the Diversion Room, where you'll have unlimited access to games like Candyland, Operation, UNO, and the new Nintendo video game made exclusively for post-lifers, Wii Walk In Place.

- Dance 'til you drop at either Gristle's After Dark™ or the mind-blowing Club Tibia™!

- Long, romantic walks along any of the 0.8 miles of shambling paths (hopefully with that fellow post-lifer who's caught your remaining eye).

Sound good? Sure it does. Every detail has been attended to, and you'll find everything you would have wanted within the walls of our too-good-to-be-true compounds. And no need to ever worry about that horrible Horde. While most Scarlet Shores facilities are Horde-adjacent, you'll be protected from their threat and influence by Señor Primo™, the security system of tomorrow, today. Luxury *and* safety go hand in almost-a-hand here.

Oh—and here's the answer to the question that I know is forming on your parched lips: yes, there *will* be brains.

Post-life at Scarlet Shores—your best and last resort.

# CHANGE YOUR CLOTHES, CHANGE YOUR POST-LIFE:

## AMERICA'S NEXT TOP ZOMBIE

Now that you've taken a gander at the pamphlet for Scarlet Shores, I bet you're more motivated than ever about *Z4Z*. Your future's lookin' great, but not as great as *you're* about to look!

So what does this chapter's subtitle, "America's Next Top Zombie," mean? The explanation is simple: *zombie* is used here as slang because in the idiosyncratic world of fashion and style, zombies are currently considered chic and edgy. Therefore, please understand that this reference is simply "playing to the room," and the room adores you.

There's no doubt about it: if you had to pick an era in which to be bitten, it's clear this is the one. The incredible nutrition options, drugs, and grooming products available are reason enough to be grateful. But what you don't know is, we've saved something super special for *this* "chapter" of your post-life.

## YOU'RE GOING OUT LIKE THAT??!

 I can hear you say: "For God's sake, large patches of my skin are falling off. Why in the world would I care about personal style or

As you've been reading *Z4Z*, you may have become forlorn and simply forgotten to change your clothes. Historically, this has been the modus operandi for a lot of folks in the Transition. Fear of the future paralyzes them on such a visceral level that they become apathetic about their appearance. If you let the fear get to you and stumble down that path, however, there's a strong likelihood you'll end up in whatever you're currently wearing for, oh, the *next several decades*. How embarrassing. You do not want to end up looking so sixteen years ago.

stupid clothes right now?" Let's review your sitch once again: we're working together to ensure the Transition doesn't take you down to Funkytown. Push through your living dead-end feelings of self-pity, and listen up: your symptoms *will* level off and your condition *will* improve. If you want to succeed in the post-life, you're going to have to look the part. And people, success is *not* going to happen with you dressed like *that*!

Prior to the creation of Containment Zones, infected folks wandered freely around towns, looking for a handout or just a hand. Like somnambulant Dickensian urchins, they were clad only in the tatters of their former lives. Such a shoddy sense of personal appearance wreaked havoc not only on *their* self-esteem, but it bummed out everyone who came into contact with them. Over time, this situation took a toll and the world looked all the worse for wear—neither smart nor sassy. And so it came to pass that on one fateful day, a group of noble queens decided they'd had enough and vowed to change the world with a return to fabulousness.

That's right. The recent strides that have

been made regarding workable and feisty attire for post-lifers didn't happen on their own; it took the courage and conviction of a band of heroic artistes to make this a reality. Let me tell you a little story.

## FASHION S.O.S. (SAVE OUR STYLE)!

On a crisp spring day in Paris, during the mega-event that *is* Fashion Week, a daring group of world-class designers secretly assembled after hours to deal with the ongoing threat to global glamour. They came from as far away as Milan, London, and New York to premiere their up-to-the-minute collections. But unbeknownst to the paparazzi and fans, these designers had in fact set themselves another goal. The slapdash style that had emerged as a result of the Provo Virus had finally gone too far, and these intrepid fashionistas were determined to meet this hazard head-on. Their plan: gather in private, pull an all-nighter, and put their collective minds and skills together for the cause. And maybe enjoy a colorful cocktail or two as they collectively confabbed.

In a chicly refurbished former chocolate factory adjacent to the Seine, this cabal of creators arrived under the cover of darkness. Nine designers gathered that night, but only seven made it until the next morning.[23] The mission was simple, yet nightmarishly complex: construct flattering outfits for those who were still being labeled *zombies*.

Initially, questions flooded the room as the designers all spoke at once: How does one address the gender differences? Would a unisex look be more functional? What type of fabric is durable enough to deal with the zombie lifestyle? What truly goes best with red? Do buttons require greater motor skills than the zombies possess? And what of zippers, man,

---

23. Apparently, two stormed out over the group's refusal to have the spanking-new ensembles assembled in Singapore. And, reportedly, the catered desserts left much to be desired.

what of zippers? Could we come up with a more dignified name for these people than *zombies*? Are they available for fashion shoots? Where might one get a strong espresso at 4:00 a.m.?

So it began. As the clock relentlessly ticked ever onward, Milan's legendary Giavagi struck first with a bold, clean look for the male creatures: a jumpsuit, replete with large brass grippers and a near-Goth feel. Rougeéêëë from Nice countered with an ultra-feminine approach for the she-devils: a jaunty skirt-and-blouse combo made from a new material coming out of Indonesia that was reported to be hose-able and bite-proof. Phlegm, the neo-punk newbie from New York, wowed the crowd with an idea that took Giavagi's to the next plateau: an industrial-type, Dr. Denton zip-up one-piece with heavy leather soles inserted for the built-in feet. With this as a start, the group knew they were getting closer. But time was running out.

Finally, right before dawn and after exhaustive negotiations, multiple snits, a shoving match followed by a crying jag, and more than a few hurt feelings, the designers were able to agree upon a common look. Dubbed The Bod-E-Bag™, it was an amalgam of numerous ideas that had surfaced during the night. The Bag was an outfit that offered the convenience of a jumpsuit, the resilience of contemporary textiles, and perhaps most importantly, that special look that could, with luck, help heal the psyches of their clientele—those tortured, semi-ambulatory souls (and the design possessed a provocative name, too). History was made that morning as The Bod-E-Bag, with its cutting-edge colors (like "Red on Arrival," "Street GangGreen," and "FEMA Fuchsia," to name a few), continues to be the standard of comfort and wearability for anyone who's *anyone* in the post-life.

As dawn rose over Paris that day, so too was it the dawn of a new era for post-lifer fashion. Seven brave souls gave it their all so that society could once again ascend to even greater heights of magnificence.

## LIVES OF THE NICHE AND FAMOUS

Once word hit the marketplace about the success of The Bod-E-Bag, it wasn't long before other top designers and retailers got into the living-dead game. Sales figures proved the post-lifer demographic had been overlooked and under-courted. Fortunately, that's now been resolved, and fashion for post-lifers is one of the most incredibly vibrant (and profitable) sectors of the clothing world.

Additionally, since the Disaster went global, the market has become more international as other designers have gotten involved. Argentina's beloved Raoul 12 recently entered the fray with his far-out ExoPolyTux™, a unique blend of resilient, petro-based materials fused into a durable version of formal wear. (Careful of the cummerbund—it'll take you out!) Then there's the conceptual challenger from Düdsk, Sweden's tri-gender genius, whose outfit consists only of a sheet of plastic and a belt. Now, there's a visionary! But when discussing the most memorable entries, one surely must include Betty of Berlin's recent designs involving hoop skirts and hockey masks. I have seen the future and its name is Betty. Or, just maybe, Gunn.

## A MAN NAMED GUNN—HE'S PACKING HEAT!

While the aforementioned runway luminaries have eked out their respective corners of the sky, the man who leads the charge is designer Jim Gunn, distant cousin to the noted TV personality and beloved fashion wonk. Last year, Jim set the fashion world ablaze with the debut of his stunning line of clothing, ReAnimate Guys™ and ReAnimate Gals™. Previewed simultaneously in the April issues of *ZQ* and *Dedbook*, the cumulative reaction to these brands has bowled over critics and consumers alike. And with automatic stamp approval, post-lifers are snapping up these groovy garments like bacon from a breakfast bar.

Guys, here's a little secret I bet you didn't know: chicks dig the living dead! I don't need to tell you that babes go for "bad boys." Oh sure, gals act as if they prefer nice guys, but we all know the real story. It takes one random ruffian to look their way and *snap*!—their hearts are aflutter, as they start maxing out their credit cards buying booze and baubles from the Sharper Image for that special Rebel Without a Job.

You, too, could get in on that action, because in this case your bad-boy appeal will be amplified to well past "11." Lucky for you that ReAnimate Guys has the goods to enhance your newbie naughty image. Believe me, over time you'll learn to deal with the steamy reaction you'll get from the dames. ReAnimate will make you badder than you ever imagined, with looks to boggle the remainder of your minds—everything from debonair pleathers, fishnet T-shirts, and snappy rubber vests to modified denim wear (with Velcro in all the *right* places). These separates will play a major role in the swinging lifestyle of this season's post-lifer on the go. And, best of all, the whole line is ready and waiting at your nearby Quali-Ko. ReAnimate—guise for the guys.

Not to worry, gals—no one's forgotten you. While Jimmy and Joey Post-Lifer are wooing you with their smokin' threads, you'll be getting your own makeover to complement your ever-diminishing frame. That's right, no more futzing around with dresses, tops, or pants that keep falling off. You say that size 2 you just bought doesn't fit anymore and there weren't any zeros on the racks? Get this: ReAnimate Gals offers sizes that go well into the negative numbers! But it doesn't stop there:

ReAnimate Gals has licensed The Bod-E-Bag design, creating its own version for those sultry nights out on the town or deep in the woods. It's the ultimate in comfort and convenience; zip it up and you're ready to go. And the patented Nano Fiberz™ are oh so EZ to scrub at the end of the day. With ReAnimate Gals, it won't be long before your friends are asking, "*Who* are you wearing?" and they *won't* be talking about the bloodstains on your blouse!

## HOLY FRIJOLES, IT'S MADE OF *WHAT*??!!

Recently there's been an astonishing arrival on the post-life apparel scene. In a futuristic scenario where biotech meets the runway, a company called PlankTog, located in the remains of the Silicon Valley, has come out with what they refer to as The Living Suit™. In order to study the efficacy of the product before it's released to the general public, PlankTog is limiting the initial testing of this suit to the post-lifer community. This is one killer app and a hell of an opportunity for you.

Here's how it works: PlankTog scientists created a genetically engineered plankton, enhanced and customized for a host of specific uses. This took the better part of a year in failed attempts, but, once successful, they then figured out a way to drop the über-sludge inside a stylish, breathable membrane that has the look and feel of a poly-cotton blend. If you're a guy, this membrane consists of a flight suit of sorts; if you're a woman, it's a mid-length dress.

But here's where it gets truly insane: the enhancements to the plankton include such bonuses as a greatly increased lifespan, a heartier constitution, limited map skills, and the ability to excrete a type of salve that, by its nature, soothes the skin and benefits the body. In addition, by pressing a node on the inside collar of The Living Suit, the jacked-up plankton are administered a subtle electrical jolt (something you'll never feel) produced from The Suit's own microbattery. As a result, this shock makes the little devils simultaneously secrete their beneficial slop, the collective unguent is released by The Suit, absorbed into the skin, and gives the wearer a nourishing spritz.

## ISSUES WITH THE SUIT

Since the release of this edition of *Z4Z*, there have been only two issues of minor significance related to The Living Suit. If the membrane of The Suit is somehow accidentally gashed or punctured (which is not easy to do), the syrupy bio-gunk will leak and reportedly packs quite the stank. Gratefully, a krill patch is in development to deal with this trouble-ticket issue. In turn, it has been observed that certain individuals abuse The Suit by pressing the node too frequently and over-shocking the plankton. This *cannot* be done. There are strict warnings in The Suit's manual as well as cautionary reports circulating throughout the media. Why? The practice of over-shocking results in the not-so-sea monkeys being forced into a near-diarrhetic state. Understandably, this can lead to extremely P.O.'d plankton. (You do *not* want to get on their last nerve.) In the two most publicized cases where such abuse occurred, The Suit turned on its owners and briefly pinned them to the floor. While neither party was permanently harmed, the psychological damage was considerable and, in both cases, The Suits had to be put down.

You *do* understand the ramifications of this, right? Such a therapeutic item might possibly make you healthier and help preserve your semi-dubious hide. The Living Suit is destined for greatness and gets a big thumb's up from this author.

 If you choose to participate in the study that PlankTog is conducting, you'll be issued your proper suit model gratis (sorry, no cross-dressers allowed). Once The Living Suit is donned, expect to wear it for four weeks nonstop; PlankTog is seeking a high level of commitment. Because of the possible inconvenience during this time, they're offering generous stamp bumps based on the degree of your participation. In turn, other perks will be administered for specific kindnesses shown to The Suit. Consider being a part of this study.

But again, no over-shocking.

## ❧ CONTEMPLATE *THIS*, THOREAU! ❧

Get a load of this quote from Henry David Thoreau: "Distrust any enterprise that requires new clothes." Right. Damn easy to do when you live on a *frickin' pond*. Get a grip, Hank Dave. Here's a dose of reality for ya: if the Horde had ever wandered into Walden and started munching on your solitary butt, you would've thought a whole lot differently about that "enterprise" notion. Know what I'm sayin'?

## POST-LIFE IS AN ENTERPRISE!

So in order to help you dress for success in the coming years while simultaneously pissing off Thoreau, I've recruited *Dedbook* editor-at-large and fashion pundit Bobby Florentina to add his two stamps. Bobby, make it work!

*This is such an interesting challenge. The most significant issue we're dealing with here is body type, which is, to put it mildly, skinny. I mean, can you people get any skinnier? I'm so jealous. I've been trying to lose these same three pounds for years; I think something's stuck in there!*

*Anywho, of course one can choose to go with designer labels and wear the ready-made stuff you've read about here, but perhaps you're one of those folks who want to use your Garment Stamps in a more savvy manner. Or maybe you're looking to reestablish your own highly developed sense of style, one that doesn't include plastic bibs. This is why, after considerable thought, consultation, and more mimosas than I care to count, I recommend that you forget about anything that is high-end or froufrou. What I'm really saying is, let's get back to basics.*

*Here are my tips: for people with your build or lack of same, layering is an excellent idea. Layering can help you appear bulkier and, if done correctly, creates a dynamic look. Transition dudes, no need to limit your layering to a jacket over a sweater over a shirt; instead, pump it up and try a jacket over two sweaters over three shirts. And then maybe a hoodie on top of the whole thing. Try it and see how very fly it looks. And listen up, boys: stay away from those fitted shirts. They are so not you. You do NOT need to draw attention to your deteriorating torsos.*

*And girlfriends, you can do the same when it comes to layering—don't be afraid to add more to the mix than you used to. This year's look is pure Russian immigrant—like you escaped from the czar with everything you own on your back. A bulky dress or three, several sweaters, and an oversized coat. All these will give you the definition you so desperately desire. Additionally, consider longer skirts and more than a few pairs of tights to bulk up and, dare I say, cover up those withered pins of yours.*

*For both genders, a former no-no is now all-go—horizontal stripes can be enormously effective for giving the illusion of a figure. The wearing of large plaids, argyle patterns, and lurid paisleys can also be a successful way to give the semblance of girth. And for Pete's sake, don't buy anything called "skinny jeans." Go for the heavier fabrics in general—wools, burlaps, and brocades are all apropos here.*

*Lastly, I encourage you to use simple common sense. Whatever you once knew about slimming looks is now history. Don't even go back there; that sublet is, like, totally vacant. Just because you're starting anew doesn't mean you can't look like a million stamps in your glitzy post-life. Play with the looks I've described, and I bet you'll find, when the dust settles, you'll be living larger than ever.*

## ACCESSORIZE AND SHINE!

While not a vital component of male fashion, accessorizing for women is a big deal. Every girl knows that the right earrings or purse can turn humdrum into holy cow! Accordingly, try these ideas to enhance your look.

## PIERCINGS

You'll be surprised to find that you'll likely have more piercings than you used to (blackouts in the forest or on the shambling paths can do that to you). You can dress up those "mystery holes" with earrings of every size and shape. Got a bunch of "singles" sitting in your jewelry box? This is the perfect opportunity to put those lone wolves to use. And, as always, keep the big danglies or giant hoops closer to the head; you don't want to stumble over anything adorning your lower regions.

## KOOL KLUTCH™

Only you can know what type of purse you prefer, but every girl needs at least one Kool Klutch. Yes, Kool Klutch, the first and only refrigerated purse. No more of those late-morning, lack-of-protein jitters. With Kool Klutch, your meat goes with you. Haven't got time for a steak but you need a little pick-me-up? Just pop open the Kool Klutch and your craving crisis is averted. And Kool Klutch comes in three practical sizes: Bologna, Roast, or Whole Pig.

## BELTWAY™

Guys, this tip applies to you, too, so listen up. I'm sure, with your decreasing-mass "issue," you've noticed it's hard to find a belt that fits properly. I don't care how handy you are, you can't keep punching holes in your old belts or resort to using bungee cords. And no going all Jethro on us, either! That's why you could stand to have one of the new belts from Beltway with InfiniFit Technology™. If you really want to keep your pants up or make that dress look just right, *these* are the belts for you. Beltway—a waist is a terrible thing to waste.

## CORRECTO™ SHOES

Lastly, post-life can play havoc with foot health. Men and women alike complain about how their old shoes don't fit anymore. That's because during the Transition your feet undergo serous changes. The physiological twisting, flattening, and "shedding" that routinely occur is not accommodated by regular footwear. Correcto offers a number of styles and colors for both sexes, and they're all produced with that gloriously comfy Footfoam material that fills in whatever you're missing. Even the ladies will find they can wear heels again if they're made by Correcto—where trendy meets orthopedic.

# DRESSED TO KILL!

You now have quite a few options for making your fashion statement personal. My suggestion is, choose one approach and run (or limp) with it. But do *something*; that tank top is getting really rancid, and your shorts appear to be leaking. It's true: by making the effort to make *yourself* look better, everyone else will look better, too.

 No, really, your shorts are leaking

# GOSH, DID SOMEONE SAY "SEX"?

Look at you: all dressed up with *somewhere* to go! And that somewhere would be the next chapter, where you'll find the steamiest stuff you'll ever lay your eye on. It's time to polish up your retention skills, because you'll want to preserve as much of this erotic info as possible.

# THE KOMA SUTRA:

## WAKE UP YOUR SEX LIFE!

By now you should be buzzed from the meds like a *perro grande*, gorged on fine processed food, in improved physical shape, and maybe even seeing signs of an emerging "one-pack." You're well groomed, well dressed, and able to bust a move with the best of 'em. So what could you possibly be lacking? What is that *one* missing component that would put more zest into your life? Survey says: "SEX!" *Ding*!

Metabolically speaking, you recently took one hell of a blow. It's okay to admit it. For a while there, when the fever was at its worst, you thought you saw Jesus and Joan Rivers in your kitchen, scarfing down a couple of Lean Pockets. That was not good.

It's because of the severity of that "body blow" that *Z4Z* progresses in the manner it does—steadily and methodically rebuilding you. As a result, I'm happy to report that you're finally ready for adventures of the carnal kind—those sensuous scenarios that involve another person (or more if that's how you swing; *Z4Z* makes no judgments).

I bet you thought your lascivious life was gone altogether. No way, José. You're a survivor, and as long as you've got at least two active nerve endings, we're gonna rub 'em together to make some sparks!

## STIFF COMPETITION

This chapter won't be nearly as much fun if you're flying solo. Capiche? So when you're ready to enter the marketplace and meet one or more new companions (for tawdry afternoons and irresponsible rendezvous), I've got *just* the company for you. Stiff Competition is *the* dating service for post-lifers, with a stunning 99.2 percent success rate. How do they achieve such notable numbers? Maybe it's their short-term membership option. Or maybe it's their weekly Meat n' Greet Get-Togethers that make "speed dating" look like a slo-mo sequence. Or perhaps it's Stiff Competition's realistic, down-to-earth approach as represented in their slogan: "When you just want some." Due to Stiff Competition's "casual" methodology, members know that the emphasis is less about mates and more about *mating*. And if you're a newbie, you'll be more popular than you can imagine; the members will literally be all over you!

*Enough already* with those deep, heavy connections that plague love affairs. Stiff Competition is not about depth. This doesn't mean that you can't or won't have meaningful relationships in the post-life, but it *is* likely that they won't mean quite as much. So whatever your preference—gay, straight, tri, or bi—consider giving this dating service a try. You'll be amazed at how many post-lifers are out there waiting to find someone just like them, but peppier!

## SOME AGONY, SOME ECSTASY

Once you're ready to go on the hunt, don't assume that everything (i.e., your physical prowess) is going to be as impressive as it was; that would be foolish. Right now your body is in such a state of flux, you're lucky your naughty parts are working at all. That said, there's no reason why you can't have a thrill or three with your partner or partners of choice. Life is shorter than ever, and sex is a beautiful thing, even in an airport bathroom stall.

Please know, though, that upon reentry, you can't expect too much at first. Take things slowly. Here are a few pointers:

## FOR THE DUDES

- Remember what we said earlier about babes digging the bad boys? Know this going in (so to speak): you *will* be getting more poontang than ever, but your erections will take a bit longer. Okay, I lied—a lot longer. For what it's worth, I'm not even going to define how long you might actually need to get boner-ready, because, knowing you, you'll figure out a way to develop performance anxiety before you *even* perform.

- Recognize that your wiener is experiencing its own Transition and doing the best it can. Cut it some slack, Jack. And does the word "breakage" ring a bell? For reasons enumerated earlier, do *not* take erectile dysfunction pills anymore. All "pharma-latio" products will have to be nonprescription, but rest assured, even without the E.D. drugs, you'll still receive a modest level of pleasure. Be patient with your dong, and eventually nice things could happen.

- The testicles of certain males react to the Provo Virus by attempting to seek permanent asylum inside the nadural cavity. While this certainly can be uncomfortable, look on the bright side: at least you'll be able to nail the high notes in "Jive Talkin'" on Karaoke Night.

## FOR THE LADIES

- You thought guys were single-minded about sex *before*? They're about to get even more so—like they're stuck on a hormonal monorail. Their primitive lizard brains will be thinking of little else, so I hope you can accept this and get used to it. Who knows, maybe you'll enjoy the additional attention. Or maybe you'll do as other women have: become a lesbian or take up hobbies you can do *during* sex such as decoupage or scrapbooking. Why, one gal I know works with her BeDazzler as the ol' hubby humps her like a hound dog. *That's* multitasking!

- Speaking of "getting used to it," lubrication will now be a necessity for every woman. Fortunately, ChemKwik offers the ultimate in home-lubing: Lubital™. Derived from a compound developed to keep ball bearings moving in subzero space, Lubital is more than capable of meeting your intimate needs. Lube the one you're with—with Lubital!

- Finally, akin to the men, you'll find that you're less responsive "down there" than prior to the Transition. But there's an upside: according to recent clinical studies, your nipples will be approximately 525–600 percent more sensitive. Therefore, practice extreme caution when perusing your breastal regions so as to avoid fainting or whiplash.

### FOR THE GAY/BI/TRI POST-LIFERS

- You may, in all likelihood, experience a more fulfilling sensual life, which is a roundabout way of saying you're gonna be boffin' way more. As we've discovered over the last few years, post-lifers, in general, seem to be more open to all kinds of sexual experiences. And I do mean *all*. The recently released Scarlet Shores Study indicates increased tendencies among post-lifers to—and I'm paraphrasing here—shag whomever or whatever's around. Apparently gender and genus preferences become blurrier and can even include trysts with the occasional appliance. Do you know where *your* blender's been?

### FOR ALL POST-LIFERS

- You may experience a slight degree of discomfort while doing the dirty deed. Truth be told, it may be more like sporadic blinding pain, but c'mon, your body's got issues right now. Be nice to it. The full list of biological reasons why this is happening is something you do *not* want to read about. However, with proper preparation, levers, and pulleys, nothing should prevent you from deriving a speck of satisfaction in due course. Later in this chapter, you'll discover a few positions that can be surprisingly stimulating. That is, for those of you who are still stimulate-able. For the rest of you, consider spending more stamps!

## TOUCH ME IN THE MORNING, THEN JUST WASTE AWAY

 At its core, the exploration of the "realm of the senses" is far more than just the consummation of The Act. Rather, it is an

Speaking of your stint at the Shores, when you and your mate prepare for that next wild night of hot monkey sex, consider including playful clothes, lingerie, or costumes. These items will add a dash of cayenne to the evening's events, and all are available in the draped-off Adultz Only section of the Shores' gift shops. There are only two prohibitions that the Shores Admin need to relay: 1) no medical costumes of any sort, because that can get confusing to your providers; and 2) no giant, crotchless furry animal costumes, because that's wrong in more ways than we have time to address.

expression of affection that builds like a sonata and leads to a crescendo of the sacred union, sometimes taking up to a full four or five minutes.

Part of that beautiful buildup is what we know as foreplay, which is now more important than ever. Matter of fact, foreplay is your new best buddy! The word *quickie* won't be applicable to *anything* you do anymore, so get used to the idea of a "slow dance." By acclimating to the idea that the act of love will be more like three or four acts with two intermissions and maybe one of those nice frozen malts, you'll become far more accepting of the results.

As I said, there will be a slight loss of sensation, and it's entirely possible I may be understating the situation by using the word *slight*. But, once again, there's a positive side: whatever you'll lose in quality, you'll more than make up for in quantity. Post-lifers are known for their voracious appetites and not just in the Hall o' Fixins. I hear there's enough *schtupping* going on at the Shores to make Wilt Chamberlain blush!

## FOREPLAY: EXTREME EDITION!

In the post-life, foreplay is a tad different, because it's no longer an option. Those damn juices move like lava, taking their sweet time to get flowing. Since you'll already be "in the moment" with someone you're fond of—or at least recognize—go ahead and slow that reposing rumba down to a crawl. Take advantage of the circumstances and enjoy yourself, okay?

With this in mind, here are a few post-Transition tips to wet your wanton whistle.

### FOREPLAY TIPS

- Ham is the new whipped cream!
- If teasing each other with touch is your thing, a lone feather won't cut it anymore; use a medium-sized bird or, if available, a Swiffer.
- Mineral oil: no. Lard: yes.
- If bondage is your bag, be careful how far you push it. Proceed with restraint (pun intended). You'd hate to have a limb pulled off. Messy and a true groove-kill.
- She used to love rose petals flung onto her sheets; now try BacoBits instead. She'll be in your thrall.
- And for the ladies: just before bedtime, dab a bit of veal behind your ears. He won't know what hit him!
- You kinkazoids who are into "discipline" should avoid veering in that direction. Really—the last thing you need is to add to your pain threshold.

- Asking your lover to talk dirty (or at all) may be disappointing. Growling and hissing are far easier to manage for most post-life partners and can be every bit as exciting. Let these guttural forms of self-expression lead you to new heights of ecstasy, even if, on occasion, they sound hostile or ridiculous. Role-play a little: "Ooooo, you're the angry zombie and I'm the hapless victim!" sort of deal.

- If you used to hit the black market for bizarre aphrodisiacs, steer clear of whatever animal parts you thought were so frickin' effective. They weren't and the entire idea is beyond creepy.

- All oral "action" is still acceptable, but, again, that mouth of yours isn't its former limber self; your range of motion will be sorely limited. Yes, even lockjaw has been known to occur in the amorously ambitious. Additionally, your tongue may be a bit "loose in the socket" and consequently might be incapable of performing its prior, Gene Simmons–like tricks. In other words, that maraschino stem won't be getting knotted no mo. Be especially cautious when french kissing so that your tongue doesn't detach into your lover's mouth. Awkward!

- Chocolate works wonders under any circumstance. When you're looking for a gift for that special night of passion, check out the latest sampler box from the Gristle's After-Dark Catalog. Their chocolates feature yummy fillings and have strange names that can be quite arousing like Karmel 'n Kidney™, Bile Creme™, and Praline Bone™.

Oysters: no. Goldfish: yes.

Champagne. Of course, liquor is always an option. Use it copiously. It will relax both parties and take that considerable edge off. No one's advocating a blackout here, but the next day's inability to recall salient parts of the evening might actually be a relief. At least until all the meds are in place. I'm just sayin'.

## WHAT ABOUT THAT TONTO YOGA STUFF, LIKE THAT STING FELLER DOES?

"Tonto yoga"? "Sting feller"? We've got to get you out more.

As discussed in the exercise chapter, stretching is one of the most healthful practices you can partake in going forward. However, *tantric* yoga is an extreme kind of stretching and would place too much stress on your bod. Those intense asanas are insane-a and best left alone. That doesn't mean you can't combine stretching or a few of the adapted asanas from earlier in the book and reap many of the same benefits. But please don't go near those alleged tantric orgasms. Your hypothalamus can't take that kind of heat and could wilt or even burst. Several post-lifers who have "gone there" have never completely returned. Yes, they smile and salivate, but they're *no en casa*. In fact, the majority of them have been placed in the Shores' Ward G, and you don't *even* want to see Ward G.

## POSITIONING YOURSELF FOR SEXUAL SUCCESS!

Alrighty, let's get to the positions. Please approach all five cautiously. Remember, these have been customized for you, taking into consideration your current state of flexibility (or not) and your ability to concentrate (as if). When a given position starts to feel uncomfortable with your mate, back off a bit. Pain bad. We certainly wouldn't want any bones popping out or joint slippage, would we?

So you know, I'm going to refer to the couple referenced in these positions as a "man" and "woman," but as has been previously touched on, this book doesn't judge you should you choose to go in another direction.[24] Lastly, it's probably a good idea to engage in the following positions on a soft surface, such as a bed or futon. Going hog-wild and attempting to make whoopee in your kitchenette or on top of a slot machine is frowned upon. Bear in mind, you're more brittle now.

The positions that follow are listed in order of difficulty, beginning with the simplest. You are strongly advised to try them one at a time and to proceed in order.

---

24. And to be fair, gender identification can become increasingly more difficult in the post-life. Helpful hint: always double-check what clothing remains; that should provide a "his" or "her" clue.

## UPWARD DOUBLE BACON™

This has been found to be a positive and sensual starting place, a ground zero, if you will, for intimate exploration. As illustrated here, the couple begins by lying next to each other, looking upward, and reaching over to employ gentle touching and stroking motions, never emphasizing one body area over another. By the way, all moaning at this point will hopefully be "good" moaning and not related to any remaining physiological or psychological issues. If neck movement is possible, the couple may choose to look at each other and, if this excites them, slobber or grunt. This undemanding position serves as a baseline to promote relaxation and can certainly be utilized as a form of foreplay. However, should one partner fall asleep while in this position, the other is discouraged from continuing the touching or stroking, because that's kinda pushy and grabby. As time passes, the couple can turn on their sides, face each other, and continue their touching to climax or to the point of utter exhaustion.

## THE CRAB AND THE BULL™ (AKA "SURF AND TURF")

As you can tell from the illustration, this is a slight variation on the standard missionary position, but one that purportedly provides better leverage for both partners, thereby dramatically decreasing rug burn and shattered kneecaps. Here, the "crab" (the woman) lies on her back and opens her "claws"—i.e., legs—to a comfortable angle. Meanwhile, the "bull" (the man), after finishing nine beers, lies on top of her, his breath a stale hodgepodge of hops and pretzels. The couple embraces, kisses, and intermittently bickers about finances. Later, after the testiness has subsided, the crab folds her legs over the bull's back, all the while being careful not to crack his ribs. As the two of them join and are locked together, they begin a gentle rocking motion, symbolizing the oneness of their unification (and preempting a mutual litany of unresolved domestic issues). Eventually, the bull's he-member ends up in the crab's tunnel o' love and, after a noisy and sweaty commotion, both are satisfied (or so believes the bull).

## SLEEPY DOGGIE™

Here's a variation on an age-old fave. This position is so damn popular because it not only allows the woman increased pleasure due to the "angle of the dangle," but it also gives the guy the opportunity to watch TV without detection. Being mindful of keeping her digestive system in place, the woman lies on her stomach and juts her posterior upward, creating a slight arch of her back and a spectacle of herself in the mirror. The man, likewise being careful of his weight and strength, reclines on top of her, facing down. This lets him admire the shape of her skull while she, in turn, can barely be heard whining into the pillows. Ancient texts tell us this titillating posture was once called "The Tongs." Perhaps this is why: at this juncture, the fella grabs his dudeunit with a pair of tongs (kitchen tongs will do, but I personally prefer the longer barbecue type) and, ever so slowly, slides it right into her love canal. If done correctly, the unit should run headlong (as it were) into what's known as her "Z Spot" and, like an overzealous game-show contestant, she should start screaming on cue (with perhaps even the occasional "Higher, Bob!").

## CLUCKING HOUSES OF CONGRESS™

Now we're getting rather fancy-shmancy. Make no mistake, the next two positions are for you folks who still feel completely comfortable with your motor-skill levels. As you can plainly see in the drawing, this position requires the couple to perform a vertical version of the horizontal hula. To begin, the woman should place her back against a wall and lean into it. Think Ellen Barkin in *Sea of Love*. Next, by placing her hand under her right knee, she should lift her leg to allow ample room for the man to maneuver his battleship into her port o' call. As the man approaches the woman, he should make soft clucking sounds of varying pitch and timbre, and offer his hands to her by-now-flamingo-like body, touching her sweetly. As he leans into her and she rolls her eyes in disgust, she wraps her arms around his head, allowing him to press Admiral Winky into the boathouse. At this stage, the couple should both be quietly clucking and are encouraged to do so until violent cramping occurs. A word of caution: Epsom salts may be necessary as part of the postcoital ritual, but beware of soaking too long—your skin isn't as salt-friendly now.

## REVERSE SIDESADDLE CARNIVOROUS COWGIRL JAMBOREE™

Absolutely not for beginners; the trapeze alone can be a handful. Carrying a pair of pom-poms, the woman climbs three to four steps up a small ladder. The man, who is sitting on a trapeze approximately six feet off the ground, places a slice of salami between his teeth. As the woman leaps into the air from the ladder, the man grabs her and seats her on top of him, pushing the sliced lunchmeat into her mouth as they embrace. With her arms and pom-poms wrapped around him, the momentum of the trapeze should keep them rockin' till the break of dawn. And when executed in perfect form, the woman should end up impaled on his love anaconda, achieving a degree of penetration previously found only in West Hollywood. If the woman feels capable, she can attempt to spin herself on his wangchung, being careful not to take a tumble or throw her back out. This position gets large kudos from the few, the brave who are able to pull it off. I would heartily recommend prior gymnastic experience, industrial-strength S-hooks, and the finest quality salami.

## JEEPERS, MY SEX LIFE WASN'T THAT INTENSE IN MY OLD LIFE!

I know. A lot of folks in Transition make that very same statement. Apparently with all the stress associated with our day-to-day existence in the post-Disaster world, the frequency of beneficial boinking is sorely copu-lacking. What a shame. That's why the post-life becomes the ideal time for you to rediscover your libido and dive back into the sexual deep end. Because certain other capacities are going to be diminished, it makes perfect sense to re-explore your animalistic, lustful side. Hell, I would.

In summation, practice the positions in this chapter and you'll begin to experience realms of pleasure heretofore unknown, as if your limbic system just watched *Titanic*. Don't sweat it if you can't immediately get past the first or second positions; post-life proficiency takes time. Build on each position and savor each experience. And don't get discouraged: the Cowgirl Jamboree isn't for everyone. I *still* have trouble with the salami!

Hey, do you hear that driving beat in the background? It can only mean one thing: it's time to *DANCE*! Break out your Freeds and get ready to shake your moneymaker! I'll see *you* under the mirror ball.

# WHAT COLOR IS YOUR UNITARD?:

## THE DEAD CAN KINDA DANCE!

After working on your diet, appearance, and sex life, I bet you're ready for the kind of frivolity that finds you, and hopefully a partner, out on the dance floor. Sound incredible? Not as much as you think.

### ❧ BUT ENOUGH ABOUT YOU ❧

However, before you shake a leg that works, I'd like to share a personal story with you. I was always one of those goofy guys who said, "Sorry, I don't dance." As a result, I ended up disappointing numerous girlfriends, each ex-wife, that mistress I had in Memphis for a while, that other girl, you know—what's-her-name in Seattle?—and a well-meaning, plastered, panhandling bum in the Embarcadero.

You see, all my life I had this thing about dancing: I was too self-conscious and uncomfortable to participate. Maybe it was my trick knee or my regrettable habit of farting near fog machines. Perhaps it was the psychological scars from being forced to "clog" with a girl in the third grade.[25] Whatever the reasons, I'm delighted to report that within the last year I conquered my foolish fear and am now out there tangoing like an ardent Argentinean. Not only have I emerged from my cocoon, but I've also recently armed myself with the proper wardrobe to boot. Who knew I could pull off a diaphanous optic orange shirt with shiny white pants. That outfit is sick!

## ALL RIGHT ALREADY, BACK TO YOU THEN

Through the magic of "equalization," you're about to become wayyyyyy more open to the possibilities of dance being an integral part of your post-life experience. Those insecurities you had about your dance-floor abilities are being erased even as you read this sentence. Even doing outdated routines, like those from the "Thriller" zombie dance, will seem incredibly exciting to you in the near future. Smokin', huh?

Not only will dancing enhance your social life by making you more "available" to your current gender-of-choice, but the health benefits are off the hook. It's been estimated that one hour of full-on conga line dancing can, in a post-lifer, burn up to six or seven calories. What a terrific way to trick out your metabolism!

## PROVO VIRUS = BOOGIE FEVER!

If I can do this, you can, too. And here to tell you *how* you can do it is the man whom I credit with changing my outlook on dance, the man who showed me what a Cuban heel can do for self-confidence—the electrifying Mr. Michael Chumley. You know him as the "Duke of the Dance," the

---

25. Six months of therapy there!

high-flying, gravity-defying phenom whose touring theatrical production of "Head of Bone" is now in its record-smashing fourteenth year on the road. Michael is a dancer, choreographer, producer, shoe designer, and founder of the renowned Chumley School of Dance in Atlantic City. Yes, the world knows him as many things, but I'm lucky to call him "friend." Michael, over to you.

*Thanks. Okay, I have but one question for the readers: What is stopping you from dancing? Could it be latent issues regarding your "accident" at the middle school sock hop? Are you merengue-impaired? Or are you one of those people who think they're too "good" to dance? Your kind disgusts me. So full of yourselves with your high and mighty opinions about choreography and what constitutes real talent. I've been listening to wankers like you my entire life, telling me I'm too short or I'd never make it out of Dublin or I don't look good in lime-green tights. Well, I'm not and I did and I do. Got it?*

*Where was I? Oh yes, there's no bloody good reason for you not to dance. In the post-life, being a social animal is more important than ever, and nothing gets people together quite like a cha-cha or foxtrot. For the men, dance serves as a great way to meet the ladies (I use the plural there because, guys, no one says you have to dance with the same girl all night). Work the room and see who or what is out there. And for you women, it's a great way to meet me. I'm kidding, of course, but I did meet all four of my exes through dancing. Your track record should be so good.*

*So where do we begin with you? I believe we first need to address your comfort zone, so I'm going to show you a terrific exercise I use at my Atlantic City School of Dance. This is a nifty little free-form routine that we often employ while warming up, and occasionally we'll try it with a group of tourists to get them off the tram and closer to the souvenir store.*

*This exercise requires only two things of you: 1) a favorite song that always gets you moving; and 2) a large enough space so that you'll have the ability to spin freely about the room, expressing yourself through spontaneous movement. Any arse can do that, so no excuses. Move the furniture out of the way if need be; you've got to be able to stagger in an unencumbered manner and hopefully not carom off the walls. I understand you're currently not feeling tip-top, but I've had students who are in far worse shape than you. My school's in Atlantic City, remember?*

*So stand, cue up that song of yours, and let 'er rip. An important part of this exercise is to not think about what you're doing or how it might look to someone who walks in unexpectedly and is immediately horrified. Allow your body to enjoy the moment. See? Fun. Now keep doing whatever the hell you're doing for another five to ten minutes. At the same time, visualize performing these exact movements on a dance floor, surrounded by other post-lifers. Picture yourself letting your body kinetically express itself without you criticizing it; muzzle your inner judge. Hold it. What's going on? You aren't dancing by any chance, are you? Of course you are!*

*It's that easy. All the rest is refinement and memorization. Get your mind out of the way and let your body speak—it's as simple as that. And while you're out there on the floor, if you happen to run into one of my ex-wives, tell her I've signed the check and it's on its way.*

## HOW ABOUT SOME HEADCHEESE WITH THAT WHINE?

Despite Michael's expert guidance, there you go again: "But I don't *feel* like dancing. My hair hurts, my fever is spiking, and I'm coughing up what looks like chunks of lung, but they're bright orange. I just wanna crawl under my bed and sleep for a month." I understand you're in a state of disrepair, but pick yourself up and get it together, because you've got a lot of work to do. Are you trying to sabotage your post-life? Well, stop it—pound down three or four more HammerMe's or whatever you need to make yourself mobile. Take a Productiva or two. Just don't let *you* down!

## NOW LET'S BUST OUT THE MOVES

Ever heard of these steps? The Pivot™. The Shuffle™. Stagger-ly™. No? I bet you haven't, because these are but a few of the *new* moves you're about to learn. And these new moves need to happen because, like it or not, a lot of those *old* moves are now too taxing for you. Spirited steps such as the Frug or the Funky Monkey could lead to any number of injuries and put a honkin' damper on your social life. Tip for the future: gimphood is not a goal. Therefore, table-topping? I think not. That furious thrashing that generally goes with hip-hop moves? So *not* good. Believe you me: these five dances will give you more than enough to keep you "busy on the backbeat."

Before beginning, please notice that there are no waltzes offered up here; there are a couple of good reasons why. First, no one waltzes anymore, and you won't hear any played in the clubs that'll let you in. Second, scientists have discovered that for unknown reasons, post-lifers have a hard time with the concept of the number three. The numbers four and five are fine, but three is a challenge. And two is good to go, so take in all the Sousa you'd like. But absolutely no waltzes for you—they can be *deadly*.

Use the step charts provided to help you learn how these dances are done. Consider putting the book on the floor so you can mimic the moves. Some of our more savvy readers have even photocopied the step charts, enlarging them so that they can better follow along. Using these charts as a study plan will be your best bet for better boogieing. Here we go!

## THE PIVOT

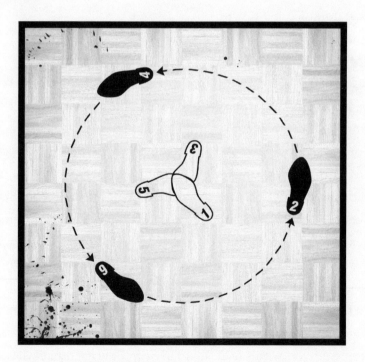

We're intentionally keeping the moves undemanding at first in order to make sure that no novices get hurt. For you former roundball players, this move should have a familiar feel. Keeping your knees slightly bent and one leg stationary (assuming you can), pivot your other leg slowly around so that the end result is that you've moved in a circle. Easy, huh? Now muster up the motor skills and, while still Pivoting, throw in simple arm motions like clapping or finger snapping. Once you do, I guarantee that you'll look like a full-blown Hasselhoff out on the floor! So go ahead, choose a tune to help you get your groove on, and when you're comfortable with The Pivot, try the next step.

## THE SHUFFLE

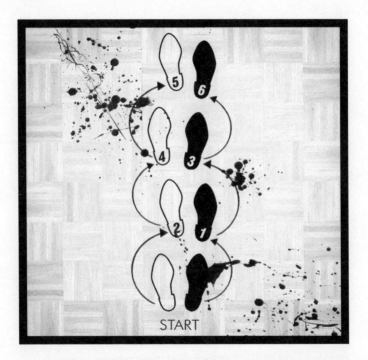

I'm sure you're familiar with Rick Ghastly's recent smash hit single, "Do The Shuffle." Well, now *you* get to do that dance too! The Shuffle's somewhat similar to the Spanish *paso doble* yet so very different. This is more of a "disco walk" than anything else; it almost resembles the Electric

Slide, but it's even more sophomoric. To begin Shuffling, assume the same starting position as The Pivot, but this time walk slowly and confidently to the beat. Remember not to raise your feet too far from the floor, because that's part of the look of this dance, hence its name. Additionally, on every fourth step, gently thrust your hips a bit to one side. Don't go overboard and fracture your pelvis, okay? And no dislocations on my shift. The Shuffle is a popular choice for a lot of post-lifers, and you'll be seeing quite a bit of it, especially at Gristle's After Dark.

## STAGGER-LY

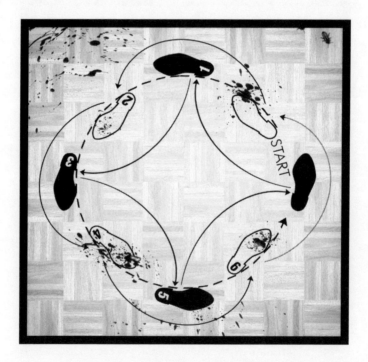

Everyone always thinks this step is based on the old blues tune of almost the same name. While a little "pimp" attitude sure can go a long way, this dance has nothing to do with the song. (However, if wearing a mustard-yellow fuzzy hat makes you feel more expressive, then carry on, bro.) Simply put, Stagger-ly is a combo platter of The Pivot and The Shuffle. Begin by assuming the same position you've used for the previous two steps. Now, in tempo, move your legs side to side, stepping forward. As you do, direct your steps to the left or the right so that, as in The Pivot, you end up Stagger-ly-ing in a circle. Again, don't forget to throw in a little upper-body motion such as pointing or flailing. Way to get down with your bad self! You're a regular dancing machine. Now go have a festive time from dusk 'til dawn.

## ROCKING HORSE ROCK™

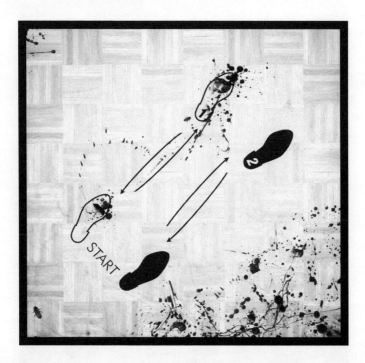

The biggest obstacle to correctly performing the Rocking Horse Rock involves your being able to walk backward. I know this sounds formidable because of your pervasive inner-ear balance issues, but you'll get used to it. From our same starting stance, position your arms as if you're holding onto the reins of a horse. Now, to the beat, take one step forward to the left then one to the right. Wait two beats and then reverse this process, taking one step backward to the right, then another to the left. If you haven't toppled over, you should be right back where you started, all the while "pulling the reins." Once you get these moves down, you can add a little drama by moving your torso from side to side. That's the rocking part! This dance will give you one hellacious workout, especially if done in a group. So be ready, Betty, to get sweaty. It's everything you ever liked about line dancing with none of the complexity!

## THE VIRGINIA SURREAL™

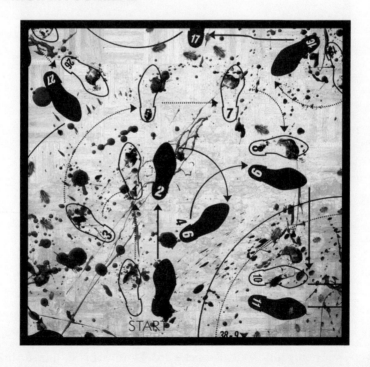

I can't even believe a square dance routine has to be included here, but I'm told this is THE current trend at the Shores' lounges, Gristle's After Dark, and Club Tibia. Post-lifers are glomming onto square dancing in record numbers, so I'm obliged to embrace it. This time you'll absolutely need a dance partner, so make sure you can find one who is willing to wear the obligatory madcap outfits. Despite the step chart shown here, the dance really can't be fully illustrated, because it depends on a "caller," usually an odd fellow who growls into the mike in a nasally, unintelligible manner, employing obscure words and phrases such as "do-si-do," "alamande right," and "ladies in, men sashay." Yeah, sashay. (The secret about square dancing is that no one understands what the hell the caller is saying, so they just enthusiastically thrash around.) It's recommended that you merely imitate how everyone else is floundering and not get frustrated. Swing your partner now and then—you'll look convincing enough. And please resist the urge to bite your partner or tie a kerchief around your neck.

## YOU'LL ONLY GET BETTER IF YOU PRACTICE

So now that you've learned a few dance steps, you have to get out there and practice. Don't fret; there'll be plenty of opportunities for you to join the others out there wobbling about on the dance floor. Hint: pay attention to the weekly theme nights at Club Tibia or Gristle's After Dark.[26] But wherever you end up and regardless of your skill set or preferences, try to find one dance that strikes your fancy and milk it for all it's worth!

---

26. For example, Thursdays at Club Tibia is '80s Night, where bad hairdos can get you a door prize (think Flock of Seagulls), and you can twist away your Monday nights at Gristle's Bloodbath A-Go-Go.

It will also behoove you to check with your activities director for what's scheduled. Certain Shores facilities have been known to host glamorous ballroom contests and, OMG, Ms. Marilu Henner has been known to show up to judge. You *can't* miss that!

## TIME FLIES WHEN YOU'RE HAVING FUNK

Hey, where does the time go? Dancing makes the hours fly by, and that's all well and good, but you don't have a lot of hours left. That sand is streaming out of the conceptual hourglass, my pretty, at an ever-increasing rate, so let's finish this chapter as quickly as possible. I tell you what: I promise to do more on my end to pick up the pace, shorten my remarks, and even leave out entire concepts. Your brain cells are flying off the mental exit ramps like there's a SigAlert on the 405. *Ándale*, babe.

## NO ONE'S TRYING TO SCARE YOU

Next up, another "Tales from the Horde." Be forewarned: this one's darker. The purpose here is to underscore the importance of steering clear of all Horde-like behavior. And if a Horde member ever starts howling at you, remember to plug your remaining ear and hum loudly!

After the story, you and I will go on a vision quest of sorts. We'll ascend into the spiritual realms of the post-life and explore "human" consciousness, making that Chopra guy look like a piker. If all goes well, we may even take a crack at astral projection, but will, of course, not attempt it during rush hour. Ethereal gridlock is a bitch.

# INTERLUDE

## ⚘ TALES FROM THE HORDE: ⚘

# BLACK MEAT

While reading this story (based on true events, I might add), I must ask you once again to observe the level of rudeness of which the Horde is capable. Tragically barbaric. Let's face it, they're just not our kind...

*Blood boils in veins. The shriek that will not emerge. Visions: gnashing and tendons. The long, slow walk of all that is. Exhaling, focusing on what offers the feeding. Vacuum of thought and emotion. Comfort of clawing, pulling flesh from a fresh kill. To never sleep again.*

We were so close to the outside edge of the Containment Zone, we could hear the Horde hissing. They knew we were there and were letting us know. It's times like these when I understood how applicable their name is—when they get riled up, the Horde sounds like locusts. Most everyone gets creeped out by the sound, myself included. Contrary to what scientists and the government want us to believe, I think the Horde knows the hissing rattles us. I'm telling you, there's more going on in their rotting heads than what the so-called experts think.

On this particular day, we were beginning repair work along a 27-mile stretch of the FortiFence, the thick vinyl structure that defines the outermost defense of the Zone (except where mine fields were laid out in select locations). There were six of us on the crew and we arrived in two trucks. By now, my company had been employed as a federal Containment Zone maintenance contractor for a few years. For this assignment, the area on which we were focused had recently been hit by a large hailstorm and, consequently, the fence had incurred significant damage. This was a storm for the history books: a freakish front had plowed into the area and generated hailstones the size of grapefruits. I'd seen footage of the damage, but when viewed in person, it was quite a sight. The storm had smacked the shit out of the FortiFence. Part of the destruction was strictly cosmetic, but up and down the length of where I stood, I spotted dozens and dozens of holes bigger than my fist. Punched all the way through, these openings provided a series of major peepholes for anyone on either side of the fence. And the Horde, of course, was taking full advantage of this phenomenon.

*Them. Out there. Outside the white wall. We smell them. Taste them. Black meat. Six. With tools. Odor of oil; father of fire. Them. Blood summons us; we scan. The feverish smaller male will fall quickly. We know it. We are blank but not void. We walk to the wall and wait. And wait.*

The Horde—or "the decomps" as we called them—were at the wall, standing and staring on the other side and still hissing away. I swear, their presence alone could burn a hole in you. I felt a bona fide sensation of malice, too, and I was a good ten yards from the fence. Then it occurred to me that maybe that sensation was just my stomach growling.

On that day, I had two idiots assigned to my group. The shorter one, Lem, showed up with the flu and seemed like he'd be useless. And the youngest kid, Emil, was too eager for his own good; I know from experience that unchecked exuberance can get someone hurt. I figured I'd minimize the impact of the two maroons by assigning them to separate crews, making them do the grunt work like lugging tools or manning the generator.

We were lucky. I'd recently made a large score by getting the Feds to once more loan us a Pluggo, a device designed for jobs like this. The gizmo resembled a giant, powered caulk gun that fired blobs of hot plastic adhesive in various sizes, perfect for FortiFence patch jobs. The Pluggo was a godsend because up until last year, whenever guys had to repair a piece of fence, it was done at arm's length from the decomps, which always made it a dicey prospect. Now my guys could safely stand thirty or so feet back from the barrier, aim, fire, and let the machine do the bulk of the work. This would be the fifth time we'd used the Pluggo and it made all of our lives a hell of a lot easier.

*Chemical smell. Like the white wall. Outside. Smell burns holes in head. Heat, noise. Them. The smaller one farthest away. I taste sweat on the one in front. Noise and heat at the wall. Lower portals close.*

As usual, the Pluggo unpacked quickly; one truck held the device and another the supplies. Once the device was erected and loaded with the forty-pound cartridge of goo, I fired up the generator and the beast hummed into action. I let the two guys who'd used it before operate it; this was not a time to be hotdogging. The lead guy, Dave, was sweating like a farmer but appeared to be ready to rock. With a signal from me, the repair job began.

As I stood and supervised the scene, I thought about how bizarre my life's been ever since I started working so close to decomps. I had enough experience now that I possessed a healthy respect for them. By that I mean, whatever the hell they are, I take them very seriously. I've come to believe that when treading their ground, speak softly and carry a big glue gun.

Unfortunately, I've had a hard time instilling that same sense of caution into most of the other guys. Maybe it's a macho thing—some men are born to be fools and find ways to get cocky at all the wrong moments. Before I started my own company, I'd been on crews where we lost members for that very reason—one guy would get the idea he could taunt or ignore a decomp, and he'd get nailed by a random free-ranger. The possibilities for stupidity are seemingly endless.

*The long, slow walk along the wall. Portals fade. Heat and odor from Them. Blood beneath the surface. Past the chemical smell. Higher row of portals. We wait.*

The Pluggo crew was on their fourth cartridge and moving down the fence line at a nice clip. Then I heard the device cycle down as Dave set the safety. He yelled to me as he pointed at the fence, and I turned to see why he'd stopped. On one entire section of the fence there was a perfectly straight line of holes, about three-fourths of the way up, punched through, each one within mere inches of another, not quite touching. The row of holes was about twenty-five feet long. The odds that this happened as a result of the storm were beyond calculation, and yet these holes looked like all the others. What the hell? I knew hail couldn't fall in a line like that. I gave Dave a look and he shrugged back. Then I walked over within a foot of the row and gave it the once-over. I could hear Horde members shuffling and buzzing on the other side. Shaking my head, I couldn't make sense of the precisely placed holes, but didn't see a problem with going ahead with the repair.

I gave Dave the "go" sign, and as he took the safety off and cycled up the Pluggo again, I told him to increase the plug size by several notches just to be sure. As the Pluggo hummed back into action, Dave fired even larger blobs of the searing goo at the row of holes. Regrettably, the physics of what was happening never dawned on me until it was too late.

*We made high portals. Hard enough ice. We watch. We wait.*
*Portals fade. White wall shakes. Wall breaks. We go to them.*

I yelled as soon as I saw it start to happen, but Dave couldn't hear me. I cursed myself for not seeing how this scene could play out. The oversized plugs on the upper section of the fence had made the surface wildly top-heavy. The more cubic feet of molten goo that flew into place, the more the fence tilted backward and groaned from the weight. Dave was sort of on autopilot and didn't notice what he'd done.

By the time I got to him, the fence had broken and buckled enough so that at least a dozen decomps had threaded their way through the breach and were heading directly toward us. Somehow the Horde had known this would happen. Had they somehow compromised the integrity of that section of fence, or what?

Snapping out of it, I ran over to Dave, he looked up, I yelled and pointed at the fence and the approaching decomps. He mouthed "holy shit" as he tried to shut down the Pluggo. In doing so, he panicked, fell on his back, the barrel of the device hit the ground, and a sizzling plug was discharged into the air.

And then it felt as if everything was in slow motion. The extra-large plug made a perfect arc through the air and smacked Lem's chest dead-on about thirty feet away. It took a second for him to realize he'd been hit and for his body to register the shock, but once the searing chemical compound began to spread over his torso, the screaming began.

Meanwhile, Dave had risen to his feet and scrambled out of reach of several of the Horde. Gratefully, they weren't capable of moving as quickly as he could, but now more were coming from behind the fallen section of the fence. I shouted at the guys—"Run!"—and they did, piling into the trucks. Weaving strategically around a couple of lurching decomps, I made my way to Lem, who was silent and still except for the sizzling. The severity of the impact, molten chemicals, and intense heat had taken him quickly. I winced as I saw part of Lem encased in steaming white plastic while the rest of his body melted. The odor was unimaginable.

*Close. So close. Can smell the skin. Velvet on the tongue. Them. Distant bugs. Scurry. Chemical smell. This one ours. Blood boils in veins. Black meat.*

I made a judgment call and still feel badly about it. But I don't know what else I could've done. We had to leave Lem's body there. I mean, we barely escaped. There wasn't time to retrieve him; we had no weapons and were heavily outnumbered. We didn't even get the Pluggo back into the truck; I caught a ton of shit for that later.

I do remember something and I wish I didn't: as we pulled away, I glanced back to make a final assessment of the situation. The decomps had descended on what was left of Lem, plastic and all. I saw several of them actually stick their hands directly into the gooey pile of his searing flesh, pull out whatever they could, and begin to eat it. To this day, I still see that image when I close my eyes.

Because of the break in the fence, the Paraguards were called in and we lost the remainder of the contract. I laid off most of my crew and filled out reams of paperwork from the Feds regarding the missing Pluggo. There were, of course, major ramifications from the loss of Lem: depositions and red tape and all sorts of crap to further remind me of that awful day. Little did I know that Lem's uncle was a bigwig in the Paraguards, and he and his lawyer told me they'd see me in civil court. Great. Like the nightmares aren't punishment enough.

*One time. Then another time. Then another. Time. Time we have. We stand by the White Wall. We wait. We watch. Them.*

# TAO TE CHA-CHING!:

## A WEALTH OF SPIRITUALITY IN THE POST-LIFE

Good news for modern Transitioneers: your spiritual life doesn't need to substantively dwindle in the post-life. True, a little of your zeal may be "taken off the top," but we'll address that later.

### LET'S GET EQUALIZED!

In Chapter 1 you learned that one of the niftiest parts of post-life is the leveling of the playing field, or as we called it, "The Great Equalizer." Well, that field is in the process of becoming even *more* level with respect to business, race, social status, and, gratefully, your spiritual life, too. Baptist, Muslim, Buddhist, Presbyterian, Bahai'i? Now it ain't necessarily so! The Great Equalizer takes those formerly fervent beliefs and vehement viewpoints that were often divisive and magically erases the passion behind them. At a minimum, your standards will be whittled down so far that even someone like Kid Rock will seem fascinating. The wondrous part is, after being "equalized," you'll find you're not that different from everyone else (at least within the Shores), and what differences there are don't matter much anymore.

The implications here are extraordinary—nothing less than the potential for a world where Arabs sit with Jews, Catholics with Protestants, Sunnis with Shi'ites, and Mormons with, uhh, other Mormons.[27] We're talking about a genuine interfaith paradise, people. Okay, so everyone in paradise *does* seem about "a quart low," but isn't that a small price to pay for such a quality of post-life? It's like the McGarden of Eden.

Perhaps a number of you are actually horrified by this idea. Such a prospect has you squirming in your seat like you're about to get that routine cleaning from Ernst, your elderly German dentist. You've spent a large portion of your existence defining yourselves by your spiritual beliefs, and you have no interest in relinquishing them. Please, let me reassure you: whatever you once believed mostly *will* be retained, but will be more difficult to access.

Think of your sitch like this: have you ever tried to restore a computer after a hardware failure? If so, you know there *can* be problems transferring your old data back onto the machine, and then you end up taking it to those damn geeks who charge you too much and the piece of crap comes back with glitches it never had before. Well, that's kind of how it will be for you—in "restoring" your data for the post-life, there may be a teensy-weensy bit of degradation. Make sense? You betcha!

## A LITTLE SOMETHING FOR THE HEATHENS

You may ask, what about those of us who never placed much emphasis on the spiritual side of life? Perhaps you're an agnostic or an atheist or a telemarketer and your higher power is not an issue. Instead, you

---

27. Certainly everyone associated with the Shores is touched that said Mormons have developed their Post-Lifer Underwear Outreach Program.

believe in things like the "universe" or evolution or a sub-Saharan goddess named Randi.[28] Or perhaps you're an intellectual type who frets about everything, and over the years, you've worked yourself into a liberal-arts-education-fueled angst-fit with questions regarding existence.

Well, here's more good news: like your devout friends and neighbors, none of this will really matter in the post-life. Once again, The Great Equalizer demonstrates its mighty mojo. As it turns out, your diminished capacity for fanatical feelings works in your favor and ends up having a calming effect, post-Transition. That's right; it's time to say sayonara to your strongly held notions, because they will, in time, fall gently by the wayside. Soothing stuff.

The beauty part is, you're not alone—you and your fellow Transitioneers are now in the midst of the same rite of passage. Before long, this will make for a very serene environment.[29]

## THE CHOSEN FEW MILLION

Let's return to addressing the concerns of the majority, shall we? If in your former life you attended services at the church of your choice, then you'll most assuredly have that tendency post-Transition. I'm happy to report that each Scarlet Shores facility offers lovely non-denominational services thrice daily for your inspirational needs. So whether you believe the Sabbath falls on Saturday, Sunday, or Thursday at happy hour, you'll be well served. And no tithing necessary—they've got you covered!

Each Sanctuary is located down the hall from the Crimson Lounge™, just steps away from where you enter the QCasino.[30] Should others be in the Sanctuary with you, please behave. You're required to make

---

28. All hail Randi!
29. Think Moonies on ludes.
30. On a personal note, keep an eye out (not literally) for Tony Tallahassee and Dusk coming to a Crimson Lounge near you. They put on a hell of a show, and that Tony is a kick!

every effort to respect others' habits and rituals, even those that involve roosters.

The exceedingly ambiguous yet inspiring services are adorned with hymns from every faith and include instruments from all regions and eras—from pipe organ to oud. You heard me—oud. The choir is a vision to behold, too, with robes of every color and pattern. All choral selections are performed as lengthy medleys, with a little of this and that sprinkled in from every faith. Following the choir's numbers, a baker's dozen of mini-sermons are doled out in rapid succession. So don't blink or you'll miss your preacher of preference. Important note to all Christians: out of respect to the other faiths, the Eucharist is offered to anyone interested, but only at the snack bar.

And religious holidays? *Everything* is celebrated at the Shores. All beliefs deserve a joyful observance. We've got all the biggies— your Christmas, your Kwanzaa, your Easter and Passover—and also a bunch you might not even recognize but will nonetheless enjoy. You know you've got it goin' on when, for no apparent reason, you're suddenly celebrating Naw-Ruz, Martyrdom of the Bab, Bosses' Day, and Imbolc. Even Wiccans get their moment in the heavenly spotlight. (The greeting-card makers have never been happier!)

Not surprisingly, the manner in which you celebrate sacred holidays will slightly shift. The Shores has found that even the most solemn and silent of occasions are greatly improved with a tall Fuzzy Navel and a game of Chutes and Ladders. The celebrants still get their little rituals—burning of sage, dressing a goat, burying a Fry Daddy, whatev—but meanwhile, everyone else gets to celebrate whatever the heck the others are celebrating. Isn't that cool?

Regardless of which Shores you're assigned to and which Sanctuary you attend, every effort will be made to make your worship experience as painless as possible. From the plush memory-foam padding on the kneelers to the "security ushers" monitoring every row, the Shores ensures a safe and comfortable service. Just try to pay no mind to your colleagues who choose to whoop it up in the background.

## TIME FOR THE THEOLOGICAL HEAVY HITTERS!

I'm happy to report that once again I've been able to gather several specialists—this time on the subject of post-life and spirituality—who have been kind enough to submit their thoughts for your reflection.

### THERE'S NO STOPPING THE STOOP!

Noted theologian Rev. Norman Stoop, author of *God Loves You But I Think You're Kinda Creepy*, has written extensively about post-life mysticism and was recently awarded a Corman Grant in support of his groundbreaking series of sermons to mannequins. Originally respected for his work with wayward adolescent girls, after the Disaster, Stoop

If you ever find yourself at the Orlando Scarlet Shores, make sure you stop in and visit the Zirconia Cathedral, the crown jewel of all Sanctuaries. It's a stunning, glistening, stand-alone structure about the size of the Spa. Not only do famous to semi-famous guest speakers stop by each week for motivational booster shots, but hip, young rocksters have been known to perform confusing pop tunes with obtuse metaphors regarding Creation. What's not to like?

found a new "life direction" on the Quali-Ko Board of Directors. We're honored to be the recipient of his invaluable perspective.

> *I bring greetings to you this day. The Almighty has spoken to me and I have listened. Actually, He called my cell phone and we had a bad connection so I called Him back. We ended up having a nice chat, but while I'm eternally grateful for His guidance, I am so not looking forward to those roaming charges.*
>
> *But I digress. He has told me that you are loved and you shouldn't be concerned about your state of being. He's seen worse. He needs you to know that He loves all creatures equally—even complete imbeciles (but He does draw the line at Ann Coulter). Anyway, He asked me to let you know that on an existential level you're on something like a "layover" between "two flights," if you catch His drift. One flight was your former life, and the connection you missed is the afterlife. Unfortunately, no vouchers will be available, so don't even start. This layover could last months, years, or your entire post-lifetime, in which case you may wish to gain admittance to the Platinum Club in Terminal B. The most important part of His message is He says you should be thankful that none of this travel involves U.S. Air—He can be quite the kidder.*

Inspiring. The "layover" concept has been a great source of comfort to many Transitioneers in attempting to deal with entering the post-life passage.

## THE PASTOR WHO SPEAKS IN *ALL CAPS*!

Pastor O. J. ("the Juice") Rodgers approaches the post-life from a different angle. Born and raised in a small sod house outside of Tulsa,[31] the Juice learned

---

31. Interestingly, the sod house was situated in an otherwise middle-class suburban neighborhood circa 1973.

a lot about the realities of life arising from such poverty. Homeschooled at an Arby's, he discovered early on how America treats its have-nots (which was strange, considering his dad was a successful actuary). Upon receiving his degree from the Davy Crockett School of Divinity, the Juice started his tele-ministry preaching out of a hopped-up Winnebago. With the work ethic of an oil lobbyist, he went on to achieve international recognition and strong ratings. Now broadcasting to seventy-three countries a week, and still from that original Winnebago, Pastor Juice brings his fire-and-brimstone rhetoric into play as he shares his beliefs with us.

*On the DAY the Provo Virus was created, a door opened to another dimension and our world was forever changed. This DARK new world had fewer KOAs and was less RV-friendly. But, like the dangerous pizza that brought ABOUT this plague, we, my friends, are all tainted. TAINTED, I tell you. And because of the Virus, the Horde was born and so, TOO, was born a Hell on Earth. Well, not exactly on Earth, but it COULD be said that Hell snagged that coveted corner unit two stories DOWN. Now, no matter how hard we pound on the walls or complain to the MANAGER, nothing will change this FACT: hell-adjacent is a horrible place to live, even more frightening than the City of INDUSTRY. And we, the survivors, must learn to live with the ramifications of what brought about this unholy situation and ask for FORGIVENESS or, at a minimum, afternoon access to a medium-sized U-HAUL TRUCK.*

## A BEAKER OF LIGHT

Next, we're fortunate to be the beneficiaries of some serious insight from Dr. Kenneth Beaker, senior professor of philosophy, psychology, and auto body repair technology at Southern Community College. Initially Dr. Beaker gained a degree of notoriety with his studies of a European village that developed a unique variety of Tourette's syndrome, that came to be known as "Tourettestein." Folks afflicted with Tourettestein violently and inexplicably let loose strings of seemingly random full Jewish names, such as "Stephen Alan Goldberg" and "Mitzi Sarah Gottlieb." But happily, with a little time, counseling, and lots of *zwetschgenfleck*, Dr. Beaker was able to get the disturbed citizens to reduce their outbursts to simple terms like *knaidel* or *shtick*. Upon returning to America, Dr. Beaker revisited his academic roots, teaching nihilism to homesick college freshmen. Later he became an expert in what has come to be known as Post-Life Traumatic Stress Disorder, wherein patients routinely can't concentrate or even recall what the word *concentrate* means. Since then he has devoted much of his time exclusively to the post-life community, mainly through his Beaker Institute of Transitional Studies. His many years of working directly among them gives him a unique take.

*They're like children, in a way. Really ravenous children with feeble motor skills. But they do possess an inherent innocence about life that's nearly contagious. And I mean "contagious" in a good way. In spending time with post-lifers, I can't help but recognize the divine in action. It's as apparent as the remnants of noses on their faces. Here's how I see it: if I am who I believe I am, then, as part of my faith, I must, in turn, bear witness to that which is sacred, around me, even when it includes drool and too many commas. Indeed, this reverence for their state of being is the essence of what the post-life is truly about: no longer are these souls bound to this Earth, where*

*we continue to suffer, slave, and are forced to watch TMZ. No, the*
*post-lifers are not among us anymore. They have moved beyond us.*
*They're free now and are, indeed, halfway to heaven.*

Bet you never thought about it that way: "halfway to heaven." That is
as beautiful as your future is *ever* going to get!

## AND AN EXOTIC DANCER, *TOO*? DAMN!

But it's not just Western spiritual leaders who have pondered the
experiences of those in the Transition or post-life. Asian poet/essayist/
former exotic dancer Bamboo Reed compiled her thoughts on time spent
at a Shores facility in her bestseller, *The Tao of Scarlet Shores: One Good*
*Internment Deserves Another*. Here, in artful, mystifying verse, Reed
shares examples of her observations:

> *The Way that can be staggered is the only Way.*
> *The words that can't be formed are usually the words.*
> *The foods that can't be eaten are probably best left alone.*
> *The caged tiger will know its prey but opt for the taco bar.*

In Chapter 3 she ruminates:

> *Not-being is the flower on the water.*
> *The lily on the surface of the pond is dumb as a brick;*
> *yet, it is not judged, it is not found wanting.*
> *It is, however, hungry like the wolf, which has little to do with the lily.*
> *Go figure.*

And in Chapter 7 we encounter this gem:

*The empty head is not as empty as one might think.*
*The thinking head is not as thinky as one might suspect.*
*A vessel of non-ness is still a vessel.*
*What is "is"?*

And this in Chapter 10:

*Beauty gets in the Way and is overrated.*
*Ugly is all in your mind.*
*Both are part of the same tree.*
*See the tree, how big it's grown.*

Lastly, Bamboo Reed offers what is now considered to be a modern classic from Chapter 11:

*A warrior, a rabbi, and a penguin go into a bar.*
*The warrior is the one who orders the drink of the righteous:*
*wisdom with a water back.*
*This is indicative of the mastery of self.*
*And cluelessness regarding booze and the company one keeps.*
*Never drink with a penguin.*

I do not tire of her work; it's consistently a feast for the soul.

## BUT WHAT DOES IT ALL MEAN?

You've been given a hefty amount of deep-sounding stuff in a short amount of time. So what does it all mean? That's not an answer I can provide; that's one *you're* going to have to figure out. But I can tell you this: as the Transition unfolds and rushes toward completion, you will find that certain ethical compromises may occur; for instance, "meaning" may be abandoned in favor of salty snacks. Those philosophical issues you've been wrestling with all your life will, at long last, leave the stage so that sugary beverages can "sit in." Best of all, any remaining *sturm und drang* related to "being" or "not being" can easily be traded for a ShuffleCraft trip to the local QCasino. What the hell; post-life is short, so feel free to cut loose and play that penny slot right by the lower-level men's room. Cha-ching!

## END HO!

I hope our spiritual contributors spoke to that deepest part of you—the one longing for serenity, illumination, and a better timeshare.

Like a landmass in the distance, we can finally see an actual end to this book. But before we pack it in and deboat, we'll take a gander at *who* you're becoming and *why* you should be proud, even if you're incapable of standing tall.

# THE ROAD LESS SHAMBLED:

## GET ON WITH THE FUTURE

By now you no doubt feel better about multiple facets of your life and are well enough to finish *Z4Z*. You are, after all, getting mighty close to the end—of the book, that is. The disgusting sweats and destructive urges can be formidable, but hang in there; your ship is about to come in!

Chapter 2 addressed the emotional issues you're most likely facing. If you can remember that far back, you'll recall that you were introduced to the 14 Habits that guarantee a richer quality of post-life. However, as was promised at the onset, we're going to take a final look at ways of making your launch into the post-life a completely positive experience.

### YES, I'M REALLY GOING TO PLAY THE LEPER CARD

In days of olde, there used to be all kinds of hip hangouts like pirate islands, catacombs, Elks Clubs, and leper colonies. Regarding lepers, I believe it's fair to say they rarely got a fair shake in society. They were not allowed access to proper health care and were rarely admitted into coffeehouses or boutiques. How were they supposed to improve their lives, work on their social skills, or get a good pedicure?

When missionaries visited their colonies, lepers were met with nothing but negative reinforcement: "Ooo, your arm's so funky" or "Golly, I guess *someone* pissed off the good Lord." With such a dreadful lack of moral support, it's no wonder there was a noticeable downturn in the collective leper self-esteem.

I bring this up because the aforementioned Dr. Beaker and his associates have completed a major study on self-image issues for those in the Transition. (Mind you, one of the control groups was composed of individuals who did *not* utilize Z4Z, which may explain their attitudinal problems.) Not surprisingly, the results of Beaker's study are eye-opening. They reveal that many people actually give up while attempting to negotiate the psychological and physiological obstacle course that is the Transition. A vast number simply surrender and allow themselves to "go Horde." Sadly, when asked, a few souls even likened themselves to lepers and were observed searching online for singles colony deals at places like Club Ded™.

*You* will not succumb to such negativity. To confirm how far you've already come compared to Beaker's control group, simply study the first eight questions from his test and the answers his subjects provided, and compare how you would have answered. I think you'll find these quite illuminating.

## BEAKER INSTITUTE OF TRANSITIONAL STUDIES

"SELF-IMAGE PRIOR TO POST-LIFE"

[DR. FREDERICK MEEP ADMINISTERING AND MONITORING THE TEST]

[RESULTS +/- 9%]

| QUESTIONS | ANSWERS |
|---|---|
| 1. From 1 to 10, what is your current level of anxiety regarding the post-life? | 56% = 10<br>22% = 43<br>18% = Please, I'll take any effin' drugs you can give me!<br>4% = Eeeeeeeeyargh |
| 2. What role do you see yourself playing in the post-life? | 30% = Leper<br>26% = Libertarian<br>21% = Playuh<br>14% = Good Samaritan<br>6% = Stanley Kowalski<br>3% = Zombie extra |
| 3. How do you currently feel about yourself? | 59% = Are you serious? I look like crap, I feel like crap, and you're bugging me about self-image? What is wrong with you?<br>21% = Right as rain since I took the meds.<br>13% = Pretty bummed. Like how I |

| QUESTIONS | ANSWERS |
|---|---|
| | felt after sitting through *The English Patient.*<br>7% = Been through worse. Ya ever been to El Paso? |
| 4. What is your expectation of the Scarlet Shores facilities? | 62% = I'm told I may not be allowed in 'cause I didn't buy that goofy book. What's up with that?<br>18% = Sounds like a groove thang.<br>10% = Anything's better than this lousy test. Can I have some meds, please? Those other folks in Question 3 got meds!<br>10% = From what I hear, lots of booze and sex. Beats my current life by a mile. |
| 5. What's your opinion of Quali-Ko? | 81% = What does that have to do with the post-life? Let me talk to that Meep guy!<br>12% = Can't live without it!<br>6% = I used to be a greeter!<br>1% = Fascists |

| QUESTIONS | ANSWERS |
|---|---|
| 6. Who's your favorite Beatle? | 37% = Well, I guess it would be Joh—again, what the hell does that have to do with my self-esteem? When I signed up for this, you said there would be free meds and orange juice. All I've been given is one effin' Advil and a Dixie Cup of lukewarm Tang. Where the *hell* is Meep?<br>28% = Paul<br>22% = George<br>11% = Ringo<br>2% = Yoko |
| 7. If it were offered to you completely free of charge, would you be willing to try a revolutionary new microwaveable diet plan? | 58% = Sure<br>22% = What's the catch?<br>10% = No<br>6% = Does it come with a gun?<br>4% = How 'bout I just stuff Meep in the microwave? |
| 8. Concerning your Transition, what would be an acceptable percentage of memories for you to retain, if such a thing were possible? | 72% = 100%<br>22% = As much as I can get.<br>4% = Whatever—it's all good.<br>2% = Any amount as long as it allows me to forget 8th grade phys ed. |

Do you see how much progress you've already made? You clearly have a more upbeat outlook than most of the losers in the Beaker study.

## BUT NAMES CAN NEVER HURT YOU

By the end of the second day of the Transition, statistics show that more than likely you're still wrestling with issues regarding your current predicament. Your inner dialogue sounds something like this: "Sure the drugs have arrived and they're helping with the spasms and bloodlust, and yeah, the P-System food's okay, but I can't seem to shake the feeling that from now on I'll be thought of as, I don't know, 'less than.' People will look at me and laugh, and I may not even be aware of it. Why, just yesterday, unbeknownst to me, someone slapped a sign on my back that said 'Bite Me.' How am I supposed to deal with that sort of stuff?"

Allow me to answer. Even in the post-life, there will always be a certain number of lame-os you'll run into who won't appreciate your differences and may look down on you. Unfortunately, bias and discrimination continue to be ongoing problems in post-lifer culture. While it's true post-lifers have gained in numbers and societal acceptance, there are still those who are jealous of the many cool post-lifer perks. Now and then you may even get verbally assaulted by a random idiot calling you names like "zombie" or "perishable" or "fleshhead."

Here's my advice: let it go. I know you'll be tempted to take a sizeable chunk out of the assailant's carotid artery, but ignore such urges. These buffoons are beneath you. In the end, you can't do squat about their misguided perceptions and opinions. To that end, also please avoid the temptation to send a "Horde-a-gram." Truly, the most positive move for you is to step up to the plate and knock your post-life out of the park. Indeed, success *is* the best revenge.

To ensure that your home run *does* go over the outfield wall, let's examine a couple of options that promote a much-needed sense of peace and harmony.

## THERE'S NO PLACE LIKE OM

In Chapter 2 you were introduced to a relaxation technique called Necrofeedback. I hope you've been using it. As you probably don't recall, you were also asked to visualize yourself being calm while at the same time working on your posture and alleged breathing. Now the time has come to take this practice a step further with the aforementioned ancient art of meditation.

So how does one meditate? I can no more tell you how to do that than tell you how to catch a cloud. However, if you review the "special place" exercise cited earlier in the book and toss in incense and rhythmic muttering, you'll begin to get a feel for it. Check out the following helpful suggestions.

Meditation goes back three thousand years, originating during the time when dinosaurs croaked from the big comet and the cruel overlord Xenu visited the Earth. Meditation has been proven to minimize stress, decrease blood pressure (although that may not really be an issue for you), promote wellness, and Scotchgard your karma.

## MEDITATION TIPS

- Find a nice place to collapse. Perhaps in front of a window with a scenic view or maybe next to the fridge. It doesn't matter, as long as the location "speaks to you" and enables you to relax. This will be your sacred place, kinda like where you hid those copies of Swank when you were a kid.

- Wear loose-fitting clothing; muumuus work nicely.

- It can't be stressed enough: your body's involuntary processes can't be trusted anymore, so remember to breathe.

- Try to allot a minimum of fifteen to twenty minutes to your practice. No rushing. I know certain ashrams have drive-thru lanes, but remember, you won't be driving so there'll be none of that for you.

- Consider using a mantra, which is a sacred name, word, or phrase that you repeat silently or aloud as you meditate. Many people find that a mantra can be healing while those who live with the mumblers would beg to differ. A few of the "bestsellers" are: "om," "eek," "owww," "what they do," and "I *can* win the lottery." It's up to you to determine which mantra is the most effective for you. Test-drive a few and see which one calms you down, and hopefully your loved ones won't go postal in the process.

- In meditation, the idea is to let your mind roam freely, like those folks you met in the woods. And while your mind is out there roaming, work on detaching from the material world. Release all expectations having to do with your old life, especially those involving your bladder. Attachment leads to neediness, which can lead to binge-snacking. As your mind is out on its numinous field trip, try to empty it, not unlike an ashtray. Be free of those conceptual butts. Upon completion of your journey, remember to guide your mind home. Use force if necessary. Cattle prods work well on the empyrean plane.

- As stated earlier, try to practice meditation daily. When you're dealing with lingering rage issues (like irritation related to that dip in your motor skills that resulted in the torching of your Guitar Hero chops), daily meditation is a requisite. It's worth every moment, if only for the muumuus.

If you find that meditation alone isn't having quite the relaxing effect you had expected, here's one more idea.

## IF YOU REPEAT STUFF ENOUGH, STUFF BECOMES TRUE!

A corollary to the practice of utilizing mantras is the use of what are called "affirmations," the repetition of words or phrases that, like cerebral squatters, sneak into your subconscious and set up house. Once "settled," these phrases become "true" in your mind. For centuries, yogis and congressmen alike have used affirmations. Combining affirmations with your daily rituals of dance and exercise is especially beneficial.

Please try any of the following "Five Affirmations of the Post-Life" to aid your healing, within and without. Each one speaks to a different aspect of your current state—from self-image to shopping to sensuality.

As a group, these "Post-its to the self" have been proven to be effective in promoting calmness, an improved sense of self-worth, and something faintly resembling serenity. See what you think, but, more importantly, see how you *feel*.

Affirmation 1:
*I am whole and complete as I am.*
*I didn't need that limb anyway.*
*I feel pretty and witty and uhhhhhhhhhh.*
*I'll be fine.*
*Really.*
*I am whole.*

Affirmation 2:
*It is with conviction that I proceed.*
*Let all worry end here.*
*Let all sadness fall away.*
*Like layers of skin.*
*Mmmmmmm—skin.*

Affirmation 3:
*I am the joyous manifestation of all that is post-life.*
*I am remarkable and willing and ready to let go.*
*Zippity Doo Dah.*
*The past is receding like memories in the sand.*
*What was I saying?*
*Oh, yeah,*
*I am joyful*
*and could sure stand a cocktail.*

Affirmation 4:

*Yes is the word that opens the door from the Ward.*

*My provider prefers Yes.*

*The universe prefers Yes.*

*Quali-Ko prefers Yes.*

*Why wouldn't I?*

*Yes.*


Affirmation 5:

*I am one with all things.*

*Particularly that new arrival down the hall.*

*Hubba hubba.*

*I love myself as I am.*

*I am perfectly in balance.*

*Mostly.*

## ﹩ DON'T LET IT BRING YOU DOWNER ﹩

**!** You say you're still feeling blue (or blue-gray, as the case may be)? Practice the Necrofeedback exercises from Chapter 2. Review your diction lessons. Meditate harder! Use the tools you've been handed. It's imperative you remember that many individuals in your condition go on to lead perfectly productive post-lives. Some even become cashiers at Quali-Ko—talk about cheery! Besides, not everyone who's still *human* is so freakin' hot. There are untold numbers of homo sapiens out there who are already more dead than you. Really. Take a trip to Branson and get back to me.

## A COUPLET AND A GIMLET!

For one last piece of feel-good evidence, I submit to you the results of a research project by several scientists working with *Dedbook*. This experiment was done at the Chicago Shores last year and was an attempt to quantify what artistic streak remained in the post-life community. Disguised as a weekly Happy Hour Poetry Class at Gristle's, nearly two dozen post-lifers signed up to attend the "lessons." The study was led by a scientist posing as a jaded, Beat-influenced writer, complete with bongos and beret, who asked his students to compose poems reflecting their inner lives.

I believe you'll agree that the results speak for themselves: extraordinary verse in odd and wonderful forms. Brilliant new uses of structure and punctuation. Truly avant-garde. The following poems were composed by post-lifers, mind you; those who were once dismissed as goofballs or morons or "less than." You, too, can be a part of this evolution in eloquence.

Here, then, is a smattering of sample verse.

From week two (Dollar Pabst Night):

*shoes fit not as much*
*jerry says that jell-o girl likes me!*
*she told him!*
*i should buy her a pabst*
*is that a poem yet?*

Week three (Jägerbombs):

*darts are pretty in the air*
*why is the sound always down?*
*they got that guy talking about that thing on scarlet tv*
*funny and sad*
*sad and funny*
*head hurts when i try to feel both!*
*head hurts!*
*head!*

Several romantic selections from week six (Haiku 'n Martini Monday):

*her cranium speaks*
*to me from afar, take me*
*it says, hold me close*

*that blissium crap*
*works like crazy it sure beats*
*all them other drugs*

*i see myself in*
*the mirror in passing and*
*i'm looking better*

*liver dinner for*
*two tonight perhaps*
*i'll cook onions too*

*his only lip works*
*better than most guys and he*
*doesn't smell too much*

And lastly, from the course's final Free-Form Week (and ShootermaniaFest):

*i am more than what you think i am*
*just because i can't talk so good*
*doesn't mean i'm out of it*
*i'm still with it*
*can't*
*you*
*see?*
*what?*
*speak up!*
*hell no, i'm not talking about post-life*
*i'm just faced from that last round of kamikazes*
*s'all*

How 'bout them apples? Surely you understand now that what you once perceived (as in maybe forty-eight hours ago) as being a death sentence is more like a voyage into a unique and amazing world. Okay, so the voyage is not exactly a lateral move, but it's damn close. And based on those "beautiful" poems, you now know that you, too, are capable of creating such articulate junk, because you've still got that pilot light of humanity flickering within. A spark, however infinitesimal.

## MAN, I FEEL LIKE A SEGUE

Did someone say "humanity"? Yup, so let's get all plural with it, as in "humanities." Poetry wasn't the only art form that came out of this study. In various successive happy-hour workshops, post-lifers created paintings, sculptures, music—you name it. Granted, there were a few pieces that were a bit, shall we say, eccentric or conceptual, but all participants deserve major kudos for their efforts.

For example, Gerald Fisk's *Still Life No. 3*, a pencil sketch depicting several human organs mixed into a bowl of fruit, left many cold as they decried its use of negative space. And I'm not sure Sheila Bonar's "Ukulele Being Fed into a Wood Chipper" qualified as music. I found the melody overly strident, yet it was strangely satisfying. And we certainly can't omit Velour's pungent piece *Pasta!* consisting only of a 900-gallon bowl filled with thirty-five-day-old pasta. Indeed, a far cry from Oldenburg.

All the creative folks mentioned here went through exactly what you're going through, and look how they turned out. I believe a post-lifer Picasso could be just around the corner.[32]

## STIGMA? WHAT STIGMA?

As you know, post-lifers were once regarded as fourth-rate citizens. During the past decade or so, there was a genuine stigma attached to being one of *them*. But that hasn't been the case for quite some time, so you can put that worry to rest. There's been an increase in contact between post-lifers and the outside world on Visiting Days, as well as the sporadic field trip. As a result, the social dynamic has shifted as post-lifers have become more visible and recognized. To an extent, even

---

32. With a face only a Cubist could love!

a certain degree of prejudice has lifted. It's no longer unheard of for certain families to attempt to bring their post-life relatives back into their homes (although such acts of supposed kindness have generally been associated with Liquor Stamp fraud).

**!** The stigma is gone. Be proud of who you were but even prouder about who you *are*. You're part of a bigger picture now. When that first fish crawled out of the primordial mud to walk on land, do you think he moped and whined and longed for his former mud-life? Hell, no! He marveled at the change and at the chance to be something different. He ditched his mud-wife and kids and moved on. So it will be for you. Let go of your old misconceptions. Change can be a bee-yatch, but the horizon is just right over there. No, you're looking in the wrong direction. *Over there*. For God's sake, follow my finger—the one that's pointing.

And what's on that horizon? Well, after you've completed this book, go live it up. During the days, socialize and consume goods in a poised and dignified manner. Come nightfall, dance like there's no tomorrow, just like that lovely Paula Abdul. There's no going back, so go forward in the name of fun! I believe in time you'll find that your post-life is actually *preferable* to your former life, particularly if you had a long commute.

## WHO DOESN'T LOVE SOUP?

Congratulations! You're about to move on to the final chapter. It's time to ogle what others have accomplished in their post-lives along with perspectives from a bubbly Scarlet Shores worker or two.

Brace yourself for a warm and fuzzy future.

# BRAIN SOUP FOR THE SOUL:

## GUT-WARMING TALES OF SUCCESS

Still with us? Great! I know in the waning hours one's focus can lag and words on the page can resemble confusing little bugs. If this is the case, don't be self-conscious about your condition; all you've learned and imbibed will begin to impact you sooner than you think.

What do you say we go out in style? Here in the final chapter, rather than listening to me blather on, you're going to hear rousing tales of personal triumph. Did you know that, on average, for every one hundred infected Transitioneers, an astonishing 18.6 percent *don't* go Horde and manage to create rewarding post-lives? And those staggering stats are on the rise!

Sit back and prepare to be moved.

### HE LEFT HIS HEAD IN SACRA-CISCO

Randy, 42, was formerly an IT support specialist from Emeryville, California. He now resides at the Sacra-cisco Scarlet Shores and is on week ten of a clinical trial for a promising new synaptic enhancement medication.

*It not bad here. Food good. Drinks strong. Place crawling with chicks. No, really, many can't walk. Good stuff, eh? Little joke among us at Shores. Seriously, can see Horde from observation deck and am glad am not that. Looks like sad life. No coffee. Endless cup of coffee here. Field trip next week to meatpacking plant. Fun then. Shores sure better than old help-desk job. Those folks were really stiffs. I kid. Time for din din. Buh-bye.*

Randy is a stellar example of everything that's great about the Shores facilities. What follows is the story of another inspirational Shores resident.

## SHE'S LOOKING FINE AT THIRTY-TWO PERCENT!

Billie, 19, was a college student attending Metro Technical Community College in Council Bluffs, Iowa, where she had hoped one day to become either an assistant medical tech or a taxidermy specialist. (So much for *those* vocational choices.) Billie currently lives in the Shores facility in Wichita, Kansas, and continues to retain a phenomenal thirty-two percent of her former brain capacity, due to her uncompromising commitment to the *Z4Z* program. In Billie's own words:

*Shores nice. Apartment sort of like dorms in Council Bluffs but without dippy roomies. Handy having Quali-Ko nearby. Can get nails done there. Clothes nicer than first thought. Hello Kitty cute. And party big some days. Tuesday Ladies Night at Gristle's. Shooters only one stamp. Plus, braintinis cheap at Cap'n Ash's. Most men here are, like, grody, but few hotties now and then. Hold on, phone ringing. Talk more now. Texting harder with fewer fingers.*

# JANET'S WORKING IN AN ORDERLY MANNER

It's not just the Shores' residents who have inspirational stories to tell, though. Even the workers are blessed. Here's a short interview with Janet Riordan, now in her fifth year as an orderly at the post-lifer fave, Shores on the Shores, in Virginia Beach.

*Z4Z*: Janet, thanks for joining us.

*Janet: Is this gonna take long, 'cause I've got rounds at four and we've been having one hell of a time on Ward G. Mmm-mmm—them perishables up in that quadrant is cracked. Might be those new meds they're testing.*

*Z4Z*: We'll make this quick, then. What would you say is the most striking aspect of this particular facility?

*Janet: Well, the view of the beach is nice. Sure, you can hear the Horde on a calm night, but most of the time the wind and waves block out their sorry-ass moaning.*

*Z4Z*: How has working at the Shores changed your life?

*Janet: Prior to this gig, I was doing security detail outside of the Mayo Minnesota Zone. Standard stuff—mine-monitoring and moat checks. Nothing too severe. Still, it got too weird for me after the big riot up there. Comparatively, this place feels like a walk in the park, and the benefits are hard to beat: Personal Days and Bite Days. You're not gonna find shit like that anywhere else.*

*Z4Z:* And what are your impressions of the facility?

*Janet: I tell you what—I don't get to live like this. These fleshheads have got it good. Sometimes I'm tempted to walk right over to the Containment Zone, stick my arm through one of them holes, and let those Horde bastards have a little gnaw. Yup, these perishables are livin' the high post-life. The buffet is open 24/7 except for early Sunday morning when the staff closes it down and hoses it down. And these lifers get all those free extra stamps. Hey, I'd like that level of Garment Stamps. But I tell you what, I sure am grateful they keep the brats squirreled away over there in the Junior Shores, because the folks here are nasty. I can't tell you how often I've stumbled upon, literally, two or more of 'em humpin' in the hallway or in a supply closet or even in the stairwells. Damn! Take it to your rooms.*

*Z4Z:* Great. Anything else you'd like our readers to know?

*Janet: If you do know someone who's about to turn fleshhead, you probably will want to get them in here pronto. You don't want to see 'em end up batshit-crazy, out there howling with the Horde. I wouldn't wish that existence on my worst enemy, except maybe for Latitia, that slut of a night attendant. That girl is wrong. Let me tell you what she did the other da—shit, gotta run. Code Magenta up on G!*

## HIP-HIP HOORAY FOR VISITING DAY!

You may wonder how visitors feel when they come to see their loved ones on the allotted Visiting Day each month. We interviewed Lurene DeLonge, who placed her father in the Shores just last year.

*Are you kidding me? It was the Shores or the attic for Dad. I couldn't control him anymore. And I couldn't just keep him locked in his room, clawing at the door. I tried to make it work. Lord knows I tried. At first I'd take him grocery shopping with me and he'd end up either throwing himself on the butcher's case or hissing at the frozen foods. The last straw was when he cornered the assistant manager in produce. That's when I knew it was time. Gratefully, I'd gotten him on Z4Z at the tail end of his Transition. We were told that apparently the program had made enough of a difference to earn him a spot in the Knoxville facility. What a relief! I can have company over again without worrying about their safety, and Dad seems genuinely happier. There are lots of older folks on hand with whom he can grunt, and I believe he's made some younger friends, too. He might even be dating a girl now who's about half his age, but I can't get a coherent answer out of him. Maybe he's just shy about it. But he is smiling again and that's an improvement. Anyway, Visiting Day is always nice, and when we talk, I definitely feel secure behind the two-inch Plexiglas. Dad only lunged at me that first time; ever since then he's been a joy. Oh, my family and I always finish off our visits by stopping in at the Shores gift shop to stock up on T-shirts and doodads!*

## THE DOCTOR/DIRECTOR IS *IN*!

Next we chat with Dr. Bernard Linky, executive director of Patient Services for Scarlet Shores LLC North America. Dr. Linky has an impressive résumé, and, suffice to say, he's one of the "heavies" in the Shores organization. Here he shares his unique experiences.

*Z4Z:* Why don't you explain to our readers, if you would, how it is you arrived at your current position as executive director.

*Dr. Linky: It's been an interesting journey, to say the least. My undergraduate degree was in animal husbandry. I'd been in 4-H as a kid and worked with livestock a lot growing up on a farm. As a teenager, I fancied myself to be a "cow whisperer" but never got my beloved bovines to understand the word* methane. *Anyway, after graduation, I went to work at a meat research center in central Kansas. I found it to be rewarding, and after several years and numerous promotions, I accepted a position with the Department of Agriculture in a more administrative capacity. While at the USDA, I was involved in a study evaluating the theoretical commercial value of aerosol bacon. By taking that Admin job, I gained the much-needed time to pursue my post-graduate degrees. My doctoral thesis examined how school lunch programs had been impacted by the Reagan administration's act of designating Vienna Sausages as vegetables. After the outbreak in Provo, there was a serious need for professionals with skill sets like mine, and it wasn't long before the Scarlet Shores people sought me out. I'm pleased to report I've been here ever since and am quite content in my position.*

*Z4Z:* Great. How would you describe the mission of the Scarlet Shores facilities?

*Dr. Linky: What we do here is—and I say this in the most humble manner possible—nothing short of miraculous. As your readers have no doubt learned, because of the Transition their minds and bodies are changing at an extraordinary rate, and it's all, most assuredly, not for the better. But the miraculous part is we at the Shores can assist them in turning this minus into a plus. You see, once they've "crossed," as we like to say, the most outstanding candidates are filtered out and transferred to us at the Shores. Such opportunities didn't exist for post-lifers until the last decade or so. We believe we're now only years away from turning the rehabilitative corner and recovering more humans than we lose to the Horde. Anyway, once we receive a new arrival, he or she is evaluated, issued a room, various meds, and stamps, and then sent on his or her way. For the most part, the residents' post-lives become their own, and for those who are capable, we only ask for a few hours of service-related chores, the Hemo-Glowin transfusions, and a strong commitment to be good consumers as often as possible.*

Z4Z: What about the candidates who don't make the cut?

*Dr. Linky: You'll have to discuss that with the Feds. My information on that is spotty.*

Z4Z: Fair enough. I know you're busy, so we'll limit this interview to one last question: any final thoughts you'd like to leave us with?

*Dr. Linky: I would like to thank you and this book for the help you've given post-lifers everywhere. The Z4Z program has played a big part in filling the various Shores across North America, and that's taken quite a load off the rest of society. Additionally, I'm happy to announce ground was broken just last week on four new facilities—the Shores are coming to a neighborhood near you! Lastly, I'd tell your readers that fear will get you nowhere. You might be horrified by what's happening, but as I said earlier, a minor marvel is coming your way, and despite what you've heard or read, you won't be classified as "semi-Horde" or Tasered at night or end up eating cloned horse meat on a bun. Those stories are ridiculous. Oh, and the rumors regarding reinfections in New Orleans and violence in Illinois are downright absurd! So remember, as the jingle says, Scarlet Shores is your best and last resort.*

## THE BENEFITS OF CITIZENSHIP

Before we wrap up this chapter, let's hear one last story from a resident. Meet Hyo Lee, a 38-year-old Korean national who, while being sworn in to become a U.S. citizen, was bitten by a California state representative. Here he describes post-life at the San Di-juana Scarlet Shores facility.

*English not good before bite. Even worse now. This place fine. Warm and clean. Noodle bar yes. Bottomless kimchi. Soju with Liquor Stamp. Happy then. Sometimes barbecue but fire bad. Meat strange. Soju help and play nice with meds. Everything funny then again. Oh, must go—Godori group time!*

As you can imagine, there are literally *dozens* of such touching anecdotes to be found among the tens of thousands of individuals involved with the Scarlet Shores facilities. And every one of those folks, whether they're residents, medical providers, security drones, or Admin, is involved in a system that's making the world a better, safer place.

# NOT TO KILL THE COZY GROOVE, BUT...

Recently, rumors began surfacing concerning post-lifers and various Shores complexes. Such idle chitchat is little more than the mutterings of naysayers and conspiracy theorists. So it's only fair that this gossip be dealt with here, in a clear and concise way. We want to make sure you don't begin your post-life on the wrong foot, because by now you realize *any* foot is a good foot. Let's address these rumors one by one in order to set your mind at ease.

- *Post-lifers are starting to go Horde.* This is an unmitigated fabrication, and there's no evidence whatsoever to support this. As Dr. Linky stated, there is no reinfection occurring in any of the Shores, and certainly there is no mutated version of the Provo Virus coming out of Anaheim. Or Austin. Just preposterous. Sure, every now and then there are those who need additional medication to calm down, but that's all. Truly. Stories about these anomalies have been blown way out of proportion.

- *Post-lifers have begun biting other post-lifers, and the Pittsburgh and D.C. Shores are no longer online.* Nothing to this prattle, either. There have been a number of technical glitches in a few of the eastern facilities, but those are being dealt with and all the residents are fine. Move along, nothing to see here.

- *Parts of what was Illinois have been overwhelmed by the Horde, and the government has stated that all options are on the table.* Someone's been watching too many zombie movies.

Everything's under control in Illinois. Besides, why bother yourself about places that far away? There will always be a slight skirmish here and there, but there's absolutely no cause for concern.

- *The Horde has become much smarter*. This one is perhaps the goofiest rumor of all! The Horde? Smarter? C'mon. You've seen 'em—they're a barely walking bag of hammers! You can't *possibly* believe they'd get smarter. Those tools are lucky to focus on a fence let alone figure out a way to short out a security system and tear down a barrier (which definitely did NOT happen outside of Taos and absolutely not in Illinois). So take it easy—the boogeyman isn't coming anytime soon, okay?

Hopefully, we've put these rumors to rest. I swear, some people need to get a post-life!

## CUE THE DRAMATIC MUSIC, ESPECIALLY THE STRINGS!

Our passage is nearly complete. Our time together, almost done. Can you feel the excitement building—or is it just bile? I will always prefer to think it's the former. You and I, we've come a long way together in a short amount of time, and now we're on the threshold of your brand-new beginning. The chrysalis has cracked, and look who's emerged: you!

# POST MORTEM

You made it! For someone in your condition, you sure crossed that finish line in a hurry. You should be enormously proud of your achievement. And if the English language is still decipherable to your reptilian brain, I want you to read it here first: *I'm proud of you, too.*

This outcome was made possible by your perseverance and willingness to change. You ate strange foods. You agreed to take unfamiliar and unproven drugs. You were sort of able to learn novel exercise and dance techniques. Here's a big round of applause for your efforts and level of trust. But it's not over yet; we've got three valuable appendices and quite the announcement for you.

## DRUM ROLL, PLEASE...

As I send you on your way, I've got one last bombshell to relay: by sticking to the schedule and finishing this book in the allotted time, you're eligible for opportunities *besides* post-living out your days at Scarlet Shores. That's right, for those of you go-getters who'd rather live a more active and exotic life, there are three other choices. These offers were kept under wraps on purpose so that only those who completed this journey are privy to them. But before I tell you what the choices are, dig this: each one automatically increases your total monthly stamp allotment by a whopping 15 percent! How's that for gratitude? Here goes:

## CHOICE #1: A LUNAR MINING ADVENTURE AT THE COLONIES OF EITHER BILL OR MELINDA

You heard right! You could soon be on your way to the moon, courtesy of our government and the super folks at MineKamp, Inc.™ You'll be whisked away in style by Moonbus Airlines, and once you arrive, you'll have the opportunity to choose which colony you prefer—Bill, known for its hard-living, hard-drinking, old-time frontier town feel, or Melinda, recognized as the softer, gentler, hard-drinking frontier town. Either choice will be loads of fun—like one unending theme park visit! Once you've landed in your camp of choice, you'll be put up in MineKamp's own rustic corporate housing. And it only gets better: at your challenging new job, you'll work in subterranean splendor with an impressive variety of shiny minerals while simultaneously getting a great workout. But remember, this path is recommended only for those who really want to push the envelope and live their post-lives on the edge. All others need not apply.

## CHOICE #2: HELPING THE MEDICAL COMMUNITY IN THE HEART OF THE AMAZON

Now that the Amazon rain forest has been reduced to the size of what used to be Delaware, the world's pharma companies have found the forest to be a lot more manageable. Here you'll reside in jungle grandeur as you tend the enormous flower farms built in a last-ditch effort to preserve hundreds of rare species. These particular plants have become increasingly important ever since it was discovered they contain unusually powerful antitoxins.[33] As for your post-living accommodations, the tent villages are modern and comfortable, with the bulk of food and entertainment (including dancing) supplied by the nearby Mangrove Lodge. And regardless of the scuttlebutt you hear, the wren-sized mosquitoes are a non-issue now. By providing tireless labor to these farms, you'll be contributing to the betterment of humanity and helping to ensure that the latest post-Disaster diseases can one day be cured, or at least slowed.

### CHOICE #3: DEEP-SEA LIVING AT ITS FINEST

If the moon or the forest don't trip your trigger, how about the ocean? Just off the Texiana coastline you'll find the Cheney Underwater Resource Extraction Sanctuary™ (CURES™), the largest extraction sanctuary of its kind in the world. I have it on good authority that they've got a few openings available if you've got the guts to get there. What an adventure—this place is nonstop excitement for anyone who's lucky enough to inhabit the joint. Possible assignments here include shale driller, kelp rancher, hydrothermal-vent widener, and tubeworm harvester. Plus, the living quarters are top-notch, with a saltwater bed waiting in every apartment. But be forewarned: just like the lunar gig, it takes a special type of post-lifer to rise (or sink!) to this challenge. It's definitely best suited for those with a sufficient amount of remaining muscle mass and a heavy Productiva habit.

## THE CHOICE IS YOURS!

As you can discern, each non–Scarlet Shores option has its own appeal. It *is* important to keep in mind, though, that there are only so many slots available, and they tend to fill quickly. And remember, despite what

---

33. Okay—there may be a toxin or two in there as well, but it's all good. The corporate big boys are always on the lookout for weapon upgrades to use against the Horde.

you've heard, chaos has *not* broken out in any of the Shores or at any of the more exotic locations There *are* currently a few minor communications problems at CURES, and MineKamp has been performing routine system maintenance for about eighteen weeks now. No cause for alarm.

If you're having trouble making up your "mind" about which option might be best suited for you, please use the worksheet below. The Good column has been filled in, but the Bad awaits your thoughtful input.

| YOUR POST-LIFE AT— | GOOD | BAD |
|---|---|---|
| Scarlet Shores | cush<br><br>Quali-Ko close by<br><br>large Food and Drink Stamps<br><br>chances for sex<br><br>Scarlet TV<br><br>Gristle's<br><br>plenty dancing | |
| Lunar Escapade | never been to moon<br><br>attractive from here<br><br>more stamps<br><br>like pretty rocks and Westerns<br><br>good workout<br><br>frontier towns have funny names | |

| YOUR POST-LIFE AT— | GOOD | BAD |
|---|---|---|
| Amazon Adventure | flowers nice<br><br>more stamps<br><br>enjoy stumbling in woods<br><br>like wrens and camping, too<br><br>Mangrove Lodge sounds cool<br><br>some dancing | |
| Deep-Sea Voyage | ocean feels good<br><br>like fish sticks<br><br>more stamps<br><br>kelp yummy<br><br>hear tubeworm is aphrodisiac<br><br>saltwater bed comfy | |

I hope the worksheet makes it easier for you to decide.

## ADIOS, AMIGO!

We've had a lovely ride together, you and I, but this is where I get off and set you free. We've come so far, so fast, and yet the journey is really just starting.

The Paraguards will contact you within hours. Be prepared to provide them with your Identidocs and your choice of post-living assignment. And don't piss 'em off.

Now, if you'll excuse me, I've got someone knocking at my door who looks and acts a whole lot like *you* did a mere three days ago. What? She says she's been recently bitten and is looking for immediate advice. Guess it's time for me to get back to work.

Thank you, bless you, and good luck, wherever you land.

You'll need it.

# APPENDIX A

## RECIPES!

For those of you who are determined to discontinue the P-System Plus plan and, instead, do your own food preparation, a few EZ-2-Fix recipes might come in handy. So, in cahoots with several readers, I've assembled a small but yummy sample collection for your cooking and dining pleasure.

**A traditional morning dish deliciously updated for Z4Z. It just shows to go ya: brains—they're not just for dinner anymore!**

1 LB. CHOPPED BRAINS [PREFERABLY COW OR SHEEP]

6 EGGS, BEATEN

1 TSP. COOKING OIL

1/2 CUP DICED ONION

1/3 CUP GREEN PEPPER

PINCH OF GARLIC POWDER

PINCH OF SALT

PINCH OF PEPPER

HOT SAUCE [OPTIONAL]

This dish cooks up quickly, so make sure you do all your prep work in advance. Place brain of your choice on cutting board. Do not drool. Select your sharpest knife and chop the brain into small, bite-sized pieces. (And by that I mean roughly the size a *normal* person would bite off, okay?) While chopping, check for any residual bone matter and, if necessary, pick it out. Once that's done, get your skillet good and hot, and add the oil. As the oil starts to pop, toss in the onion and green pepper. Allow those to cook for about 2 minutes and then add the brains. It is important that you stir all these ingredients briskly together, as the brains can congeal too quickly if not pushed around in the pan. Now add the beaten eggs, salt, pepper, and garlic powder, and continue stirring the gleaming mass until it becomes a ghastly yellow-gray. Remove from stove and serve with hot sauce on the side.

# BRAIN LOAF

What we've got here is good old comfort food at its finest! Tiffany Blevin hails from Omaha, Nebraska, home of the College World Series and the spectacular Scarlet Shores Beta, the most futuristic facility in the nation. Tiff tells us: "When I was growing up, before everything went to hell, there was a terrific diner over by the cathedral that served a mean meat loaf. As a tribute to those better days and as part of our outreach group, my girlfriends from church and I bake a batch of brain loaves every other month and take them down to the residents at the Shores Beta. Jeepers, those folks sure do appreciate a home-cooked meal!" Bless you, Tiffany, and the fine work your group does.

1 LB. GROUND BRAINS (PREFERABLY SHEEP OR PIG)

1 WHOLE MEDIUM BRAIN (WHATEVER YOU CAN FIND)

1 LB. GROUND BEEF

2 EGGS

2/3 CUP BREAD CRUMBS

1/3 CUP DICED ONION

1 TSP. OLIVE OIL

PINCH OF SALT

PINCH OF PEPPER

1/2 CUP KETCHUP

(Note: if you don't have a grinder at home, ask your local butcher if he'll grind the brain for you. Quite often this is a complimentary service.) Preheat the oven to 375° F. Lightly grease a loaf pan and set it aside. Place ground brains and ground beef into a large mixing bowl. Mix in eggs, bread crumbs, onion, olive oil, salt, and pepper. Mush it all together with your hands (and remember, if you eat it all now, there won't be any left for later). Once the mixture has been thoroughly combined, fold the entire contents of the bowl into the greased pan until it forms a nice loaf shape. Cover the surface of the loaf with ketchup and bake for 70 minutes. Remove from the oven long enough to place the remaining whole brain on top of the searing ketchupy surface, centering the brain on the loaf for proper aesthetic appeal. (And your friends will get a kick out of the campy "brain-on-ketchup" look, too.) Bake 10 more minutes and serve hot out of the oven. Use caution when cutting the loaf—contents of the brain topping may be extremely hot and *could* burst. Goggles are a good idea when dishing up this meal.

# LOUISIANA GUT GUMBO

Whether you like it or not, every palate needs diversity to make life (or post-life) more interesting. This variation on a Cajun favorite comes to us from Constance McNeil, a housewife in the Houston Safe Area: "There ain't no ingredient too nasty for this dish, 'cause anything short of roadkill works. I'm not even gonna tell you what kind of meat to use—you go ahead and figure it out yourself. Here's what I like, though: intestines work good or any standard critter innards. For example, them tiny ground squirrels add texture. One time I even threw in some bat, and I tell you, them wings is rubbery but they're good eatin'! Just make sure you clean everything real well. Oh, and cook the living hell out it!"

Sounds like quite the culinary adventure!

1 LB. UNDETERMINED MEAT

1 LB. OTHER UNDETERMINED MEAT

1 TBSP. COOKING OIL

1/2 CUP CHOPPED CELERY

1/2 CUP DICED ONION

1/2 CUP DICED GREEN PEPPER

1/2 CUP DICED CARROTS

1 CUP WHITE RICE

3 CUPS WATER

1 TSP. SALT

PINCH OF OREGANO

PINCH OF PEPPER

1 BAY LEAF

1 CUP CHOPPED CILANTRO [OPTIONAL]

1/4 CUP CHOPPED SERRANO CHILI [OPTIONAL]

Bring up medium heat under a large 6 qt. stockpot. Toss in your oil and various meats or what's passing for meat. Brown lightly and ladle off excess fat, fur, tendons, etc. (Hint: some folks report they enjoy pouring the excess fat into ice cube trays and freezing it, creating frosty treats for sweltering summer days.) Stir in onion, green pepper, and celery, and cook for 23 minutes. Add carrots, rice, and bay leaf, and let that mound of grub absorb some of the mysterious juice. Finally, add water and the rest of the seasonings. Bring to a boil and then lower the heat to simmer. Cover and cook for 8 hours, minimum. Overnight is better. A day might be best. Eventually, serve with chopped cilantro and serranos on the side. (Hint: include a steak knife or some sharp equivalent at each place setting.)

# SPINACH BRAIN DIP

It seems appropriate to include one recipe for an appetizer in case you're into entertaining. This next entry comes from Jack Stick, a retired Florida civil servant and a man who claims to have once hugged a skunk ape. Now, after completing his Transition, Jack is a full-time resident at the Miami Shores facility. Here's what he has to say: "We like this spinach brain dip here. Good with card game. Beer too. Recipe normally call for bread as bowl, but we like skull for presentation. You will, too."

1 LARGE BRAIN [BIGGEST ONE YOU FIND]

1 THING MAYO

16 OZZZ. SOUR CREAM

1 THING DRY LEEK VEGETABLE SOUP STUFF

1/2 THING FROZEN CHOPPED SPINACH

1 SMALL THING WATER CHESTNUTS

1 SKULL [AS CLOSE TO SIZE OF BRAIN YOU FIND]

Bowl. Mix mayo stuff and sour cream stuff and dry soup mix stuff and spinach stuff and water chestnut things. (Hint: open all containers stuff is in before adding.) Let sit in fridge long time. Don't eat yet. Place skull on cutting board. Pull bowl from fridge and still don't eat yet. Scoop mixed stuff from bowl into top of skull. Mmmm. Place brain on top. Mmmmmmm. Eat now.

# PASTA CON POLMONE

Here's a little something for those of Italian descent. I stumbled upon this delightful dish while dining at the Brooklyn Shores a few years ago. It was so striking in flavor and texture that I tracked down the chef and insisted he give me the recipe. After a modicum of haggling and good-natured threats, he finally forked it over, and believe you me, you'll want to fork this over, too!

2 CUPS LUNGS (PREFERABLY PIG)

1 TSP. OLIVE OIL

3 CLOVES OF GARLIC, CRUSHED

1/2 CUP CHOPPED ONION

1/3 CUP CHOPPED PARSLEY

2 CUPS CHOPPED TOMATOES

1/3 CUP GRATED PARMESAN CHEESE

PINCH OF BASIL

PINCH OF OREGANO

1 BAY LEAF

2 SERVINGS OF PASTA OF YOUR CHOICE (I HAPPEN TO THINK ANGEL HAIR WORKS BEST)

First thing you'll need to do is place the lungs into a bowl of icy cold water to let them firm up before cooking. This will also give you a chance to rinse off any remaining lung juice or veiny material. (Hint: if the veins won't come free on their own, get in there and give 'em a good pull.) Now get your skillet going over a medium heat and toss in the olive oil followed by the garlic. Remove the lungs from the water and place them in the skillet. Cover for about 5 minutes to keep the moisture in the organs and to protect yourself should one of them pop. Add the onion, parsley, and tomatoes to the skillet. Stir aggressively, as the lungs may expand from the heat and oil. Mix in the basil, oregano, bay leaf, and one-half of the grated cheese. Cover and simmer for 15 minutes. While that's cooking, prepare the pasta of your choice, making sure it's served al dente. After draining, place pasta on large platter, pour sauce and lungs on top, and garnish with the remaining cheese. *Delizioso*!

Here's a seasonal dessert that comes to us from one Annie Wright, from what once might have been Trenton, New Jersey. She writes: "Every holiday season we go and visit my brother Gerard at the Shores, and he can't get enough of these treats. My kids are completely repulsed, but what the hell. The way I see it, that's just more for their uncle!"

1 SMALL BRAIN [PREFERABLY SHEEP OR PIG]

1 CUP ALL-PURPOSE FLOUR

1/3 CUP SUGAR

1/2 CUP VEGETABLE SHORTENING

1 TSP. VANILLA

1 EGG YOLK

Preheat the oven to 350° F. Lightly grease a baking sheet or use a nonstick pan. Rinse the brain under cold water for a few minutes to cleanse any remaining fluid. Drain and set it aside in a colander. Next, beat the shortening and sugar together until fluffy. Slowly fold in egg yolk and vanilla. Place bowl of dough in the refrigerator for one hour minimum. While the dough is in the fridge, use this time to cut the brain into cubes, approximately 1-inch square. While slicing the brain, use a razor-sharp knife in order to maintain the integrity of the matter. (Hint: a dull knife will cause an undesired "squishing" to occur; we recommend slipping the brain into the freezer for 20 minutes before cubing to help your cause.) Now, using your hands, shape the dough into 2-inch balls and place on baking sheet. After all balls have been formed, take one piece of brain cube and place it on top of a ball, making sure to center it properly. Repeat until all balls and brains have been used. Bake for 12–15 minutes or until brain juices are oozing down the balls. Allow to cool for 5 minutes. Garnish with sprinkles if you'd like and serve immediately.

## ORDER UP!

I don't know about you, but I'm starving! Every single one of those recipes sounds *nearly* irresistible.

Now take a look at the next appendix for everything you would have ever wanted to see on Scarlet TV. And good viewing to you and yours!

# APPENDIX B

## RECOMMENDED VIEWING

Programming Schedule for Scarlet TV

(all times shown EST)

| | PROGRAM/DESCRIPTION |
|---|---|
| 6:00 a.m. | **The Farm Report**—Daily updates and reports from the ag markets; barrows and gilts are highlighted, and the term "frozen pork bellies" is repeatedly used. That'll get your appetite going! |
| 7:00–9:00 a.m. | **Wake Up, Scarlet Shores**—The long-running a.m. talk show hosted by the ubiquitous Curt Crane and Sally Mack, former Olympic-couples-ice-dancers-turned-TV-personalities. Gee, they're perky! Expect numerous guest stars and protein-heavy cooking segments. Always a super way to start your day. |

| | PROGRAM/DESCRIPTION |
|---|---|
| 10:00 a.m. | **The Productiva™ Chatty Shack**—Wildly popular show where various female semi-celebs sit around a table and gab and bicker and cry and hug each other. Major stars have been known to surface here. Lots of fun, fighting, and pill popping. |
| 11:00 a.m. | **This Week at the Shores**—Local activities and announcements are posted here for residents. In addition, upcoming concerts and nightly specials at the restaurants are noted. Every week, there's exciting info on stamp usage. This show is the gateway to your new lifestyle! |
| 12:00 p.m. | **The Noon News**—Former actor-turned-award-winning-anchorman Tad Moot tells the news like it is. His hair is newsworthy on its own. |
| 1:00 p.m. | **Shores of Our Hearts**—Classic daytime drama set at Scarlet Shores with plots that involve both providers and post-lifers. Lurid affairs. Heated exchanges. Product placement. Long pauses before commercial breaks. If tear ducts still exist, Kleenex may be called for. |
| 2:00 p.m. | **Baywatch**—Back on Scarlet TV by popular de-mand, the thrilling ocean-side adventures of Mitch, C.J., and the gang continue. Keen. |

| | PROGRAM/DESCRIPTION |
|---|---|
| 3:00 p.m. | **Oprah**—Like we weren't going to carry *Oprah*? |
| 4:00 p.m. | **Judge Janine**—Quali-Ko's own senior (and we mean *senior*!) counsel emeritus, Janine Feldman, presides over minor legal disputes between residents and employees of the Shores. Watch her as she uses capital punishment liberally and hysterically. Small claims + hangings = must-see TV! |
| 5:00–7:00 p.m. | **Good Evening, Scarlet Shores**—Combo platter of hard-hitting daily news interspersed with entertainment features and madcap skits. There's nothing like it on any other channel! |
| 7:00–7:30 p.m. | **Shoring It Up**—Nominated for more awards than can be listed here, this delightful sitcom focuses on two interns in their first year of working at the Shores and their antics, on and off the job. Stephen Baldwin and Gary Busey are the zaniest health-care workers ever! |
| 7:30–8:00 p.m. | **That's Post-Life!**—A whimsical look at the day-to-day existence of post-lifers. Don't be surprised if you see yourself or someone you know on this kooky show. Like reality, only better. |

| | PROGRAM/DESCRIPTION |
|---|---|
| 8:00 p.m. | **Scarlet Force 9**—Action never moved so slowly. A thriller about the Shores security teams starring ex-NFL great Dirk Orgaard as Ace Hackman, superintendent of security. This one will pin you to your seat. |
| 9:00 p.m. | **Law and Order: Scarlet Shores**—Celebrating its forty-third year on network television, this beloved franchise morphs one last time for Scarlet TV. Grizzled detective Johnny Domino, played by Dustin "Screech" Diamond, shows no mercy for criminals *or* the hearts of the ladies. |
| 10:00 p.m. | **The Late News**—Tad Moot returns to wrap up the day's top stories. Check out his suits. Ritzy. |
| 10:30–12:00 a.m. | **Blissium™ presents "Later Than You're Allowed to Stay Up"**—Talk, guests, and comedy galore, hosted by perennial funny woman Suzy Saltzman. Goofy banter—and meat. |
| 12:00 a.m. | **Queer Eye for the Dead Guy**—America's formerly favorite homosexuals reunite for this Scarlet TV exclusive. Each week, the boys make over a different post-lifer, and you'll bear witness to every moment of the transformations. Don't you love how they fuss? Viewers, get your fashion notes here. |

| | PROGRAM/DESCRIPTION |
|---|---|
| 1:00–1:30 a.m. | **Z-Span**—Highlights from yesterday's news concerning the Horde and ongoing Containment Zone concerns. Just try to sleep after this! |
| 1:30–2:00 a.m. | **Spirituality Today**—Numerous religious leaders gather and discuss issues of the day. Sadly, fisticuffs ensue. |
| 2:00–6:00 a.m. | **Off the Air**—Oddly, this four-hour time slot devoted exclusively to a colorful test pattern is consistently the second-highest-rated program on Scarlet TV. |

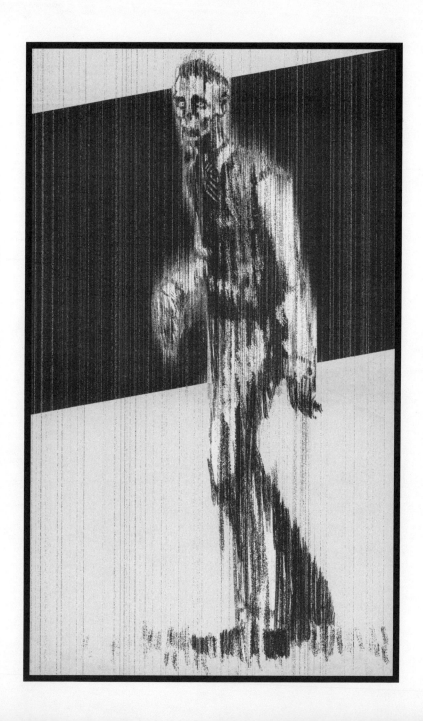

# APPENDIX C

## NONRECOMMENDED VIEWING

For those of you who used to enjoy a good horror film, here's a list of movies you'll want to avoid. Not only will they *not* scare you, but they all perpetuate many common unsavory zombie stereotypes. Such imagery will NOT be good for your post-life self-image. So unless, like me, you're able to get a few hearty yucks from how very dimwitted these flicks can be, I ask you to refrain from watching. Thank you.

*I Eat Your Skin*—(1964) Originally titled *Zombies*, this Del Tenney stinker was almost never released. Famous author goes to island, cancer researchers turn natives into zombies, the love interest is the chesty daughter of the old dude—I bet you know the rest. If you really want to hurt yourself, track down this film's companion piece, *I Drink Your Blood*. B&W. 82 minutes and too damn long.

*Unincorporated Area of the Living Dead*—(1987) A rural area outside of city limits gets invaded by zombies, and the sparsely populated region is left to fend for itself. Get set for nonstop agitation as zombies stagger down dirt roads in real time. Platinum blondes in peril and handsome guys wrestling. Fuckin' awesome! 132 minutes.

*Confederate Zombies*—(1971) The Civil War and zombies? Why didn't I think of that? 92 minutes.

*Bite of the Beverly-Wilshire Bellman*—(1981) Every bit as awful as it sounds. A portly bellman at an LA hotel gets bitten by a zombie and then starts returning the favor with arriving guests. It just doesn't work. And the flick's over three hours long. However, Merv Griffin has a great bit (or would that be "bite"?) part. 191 minutes.

*Living Dead and Loving It!*—(1992) The first true gay zombie flick with lavish musical production numbers. I'm still shocked this genre never took off. Listen for "I'm Hungry for You" and "Gimme That Head." Magical shit. 99 minutes.

*Someone Should Tell Grandma There's a Trowel in Her Head*—(1968) Grandma's kind of pale and there's a trowel in her head. Long, anxious scenes as the family attempts to come to grips with this fact and figure out a way to break the news to her. Screenplay by Harold Pinter, adapted from an idea by Strindberg. 198 minutes.

*Curse of the Whining Skull*—(1952) Short on zombies and long on dumb. An ancient artifact is unearthed and begins to complain incessantly. How does one silence a diamond-hard priceless relic? Compelling yet annoying. B&W. 94 minutes.

*976-DEAD*—(1977) Things get hot on the zombie hotline. Seventies sex kitten Bridget Callaway stars in this low-budget masterpiece. Be on the watch for her pole dance at the police station. (Hey, coppers, put *me* in that slammer!) Classic stench. 84 minutes.

*Zombie Sublet*—(1973) Ever wonder what would happen if two zombies sublet a flat in New York City? Here's your answer and, mister, it ain't pretty. Gore and giggles aplenty. Look for Ed Asner as the cranky but lovable super. 89 minutes.

*King of the Zombies*—(1941) I'm not kidding—some of the weirdest, most racist crap I've ever seen. Stepnfetchit and the living dead. If I were African American, I'd be *really* cheesed off or, at a minimum, grateful it's not 1941. At least the film is brief at 67 minutes.

*Ninjas vs. Zombies vs. Scientologists*—(1999) Thought no one could stop zombies or ninjas? You thought *wrong*! Watch these sly Scientologists strike back at both groups with nonstop proselytizing and mind-numbing readings from *Dianetics*. It's *more* than enough to take the bad asses down! German w/English subtitles. 87 minutes.

*The School That Ate My Brain*—(1987) Released in Britain with this title, it was known as *Zombie High* elsewhere. The principal of a boarding school zombifies the students, extracts a precious youth-serum from their brains, and there you go. Glad I transferred outta there! 92 minutes.

*Biker Zombies from Detroit*—(2002) Uhh, they're biker zombies and, uhhhhhh, apparently, they're from Detroit. I got nothin'. 90 minutes.

*Baby, It's Dead Outside*—(1952) At last, a zombie film told through the eyes of a jaded veteran private eye. Hammett meets Romero; hard-boiled brains. B&W. 88 minutes.

*Flesh of the Half-Naked Cheerleader Dance Squad*—(1985) Not as exploitive as you'd expect. The occasional scantily clad cheerleaders romp about in the woods, but, strangely, beneath the surface of this marginal film beats the heart of a work that addresses the bigger issues—truth, value, and all that. You know: who are we and why are we here? Oh yeah, and there are some lovely tits. 93 minutes.

*Dr. Voodoo's Isle of Pleasure*—(1992) Nothing more than an extended, poorly disguised infomercial for a crappy Caribbean Sandals-type resort/time-share venture. Yet again, bevies of beauties in bikinis, jumping in and out of the ocean. Interestingly, there are an unusual number of close-ups on great looking cocktails, hotel rooms, and banquet facilities. Zombies appear only late in the film, and I think they're hastily made-up tourists who got roped into being extras in this piece of crap. Wrong and uncomfortably long at a mere 87 minutes.

*The Skipping Dead*—(1972) Evidently the filmmakers ran out of verbs to accompany the word "dead." Not even close to being frightening; perplexing and painful would be more accurate. Cheerful zombies in bib overalls prancing about and happily groaning. *Why*? 98 minutes.

*Zombies on Broadway*—(1945) No, really—a couple of businessmen look for a zombie act to perform in their nightclub. I can't make this shit up. 86 minutes.

*Revenge of the Blood Demon*—(1962) The "blood demon" resembles the San Diego Chicken drenched in tomato paste. Not what I'm looking for in a blood demon. Next. 79 minutes.

*I Had Lunch with a Zombie*—(1991) An experimental indie piece set in real time. Two old friends meet for lunch—one normal, the other a zombie. Hilarity ensues as they order, have drinks, and try to talk. An effin' existential delight. 88 minutes.

*Someone Should Tell Grandma There's a Trowel in Her Head Again*—(1970) Hard to imagine why anyone did a sequel to the first *Grandma*, but here it is. Condemned by Pinter, it's a flagrant rip-off of the original. The family's back for more hand-wringing, avoidance, and lack of action. In this incarnation, Jo Anne Worley is "Grandma," and she's the lone highlight. 93 minutes.

# ABOUT THE AUTHOR

David P. Murphy is a songwriter and producer of two CDs, *Shining in a Temporary Sun* and Henry Perry's *Effortless*. He has been playing piano since he was a kid and is still trying to get it right.

Mr. Murphy currently resides in his hometown of Omaha, Nebraska (much to his amazement and delight), with his unusually large cat, Beany. He has recently completed his newest musical, *anotherwhere*, and his next album, *Standing on Salinger's Lawn*, will be released in late 2009. For more about him, please take a gander at www.davidpmurphy.com

This is his first book.

He hopes to one day retire to Scarlet Shores Beta. Now *that's* post-livin'!

# ABOUT THE ILLUSTRATOR

Daniel Heard is a living, breathing illustrator and graphic novelist. A graduate of the S.F. Academy of Arts, his artwork is featured in Daniel H. Wilson's and Anna Long's book, *The Mad Scientist Hall of Fame*, and the Tori Amos graphic novel, *Comic Book Tattoo*. To see more of his work, please visit his website at www.danielheard.com.